CANADA'S GREATEST MYSTERIES

Peter Boer

QUAGMIRE PRESS

© 2014 by Quagmire Press Ltd.
First printed in 2014   10 9 8 7 6 5 4 3 2 1
Printed in Canada

The Publisher: Quagmire Press Ltd.
Website: www.quagmirepress.com

Library and Archives Canada Cataloguing in Publication

Boer, Peter, 1977–, author
  Canada's greatest mysteries / Peter Boer.

Includes bibliographical references.
ISBN 978-1-926695-23-5 (pbk.)

1. Canada—Miscellanea. 2. Curiosities and wonders—Canada. I. Title.

FC60.B63 2015   971   C2015-902880-9

Project Director: Hank Boer
Cover Images: Front and back cover background © PeteSherrard / Thinkstock; running figure silhouette © decisiveimages / Thinkstock; bloody
hand © FelixRenaud / Thinkstock
Inside Images: Every effort has been made to accurately credit the sources of
the photographs and illustrations. Any errors or omissions should be reported
directly to the publisher for correction in future editions.
Images Courtesy of: Glenbow Museum: 26 (NA-1779-2), 30 (NA-1779-3),
210 (PA-3552-5), 212 (NA-2878-1), 214 (NA-1037-4); Lucan Area Heritage
& Donnelly Museum: 73, 76, 78, 80, 86; Wikimedia Commons: 13 (Parks
Canada), 16, 18, 19, 20, 21, 23, 28, 31, 45, 47, 48, 63, 103, 105, 106, 110; 127,
132, 135, 166, 168, 188, 197, 215, 231.

Produced with the assistance of the Government of
Alberta, Alberta Media Fund.

PC: 32

Contents

Introduction

~

Canada is far from boring.

It turns out that this country, famed the world over for its polite, level-headed and apologetic citizens, has quite the mysterious underbelly, both in its past and in some parts of the present day. The stories in this book are proof of that. And the 12 full mysteries and 10 condensed versions detailed in this book are just a small sampling of all the unexplained occurrences, unsolved crimes and other mysterious events that have taken place in this country. Those mysteries, in some cases, go back hundreds of years, to before Canada was even a country, while others are much fresher or still persevere to this day.

Consider the ill-fated Franklin expedition, famous in the annals of history for leaving Great Britain to discover the infamous Northwest Passage that would make it much faster and easier for British ships to reach the Orient. It just disappeared with few indications as to what might have happened to the two ships and their crews. While there have been clues found here and there, it was not until recently that one part of this mystery was solved when the wreckage of one of the ships, HMS *Erebus*, was found in Canada's north. Canadians have since been treated to up close photographic and visual footage of that wreck, as well as being confronted with the alluring possibility of finding the second ship as well. While it is unlikely that *Erebus* will be raised from its icy depths, it might still contain a trove of information that could finally answer so many of the questions about what happened to the expedition.

Then there's Oak Island, quite possibly one of the most confounding of all the mysteries in this book. Legend tells of disturbed land and evidence of someone burying something beneath the surface, possibly pirate treasure or proof that it was Francis Bacon and not William Shakespeare that wrote Shakespeare's plays. While it is not known exactly where the information about these theories came from, and while it seems, in my opinion, highly unlikely that the technology of a couple of hundred years ago could continue to defy the smarts and technology of the modern age, it seems some people are still determined to keep looking. And to show just how much a product of a modern age this treasure hunt has become, there's even a reality television series about it.

There is the story of Jerome, a man who suddenly appeared on the shores of Sandy Cove, Nova Scotia. How he got there, no one was ever able to figure out as Jerome had no legs and either could not or would not speak intelligibly. He was passed from family to family until he found a home with one family who looked after him until he died. The provincial government even paid a stipend to support his care. But while wild and far-fetched theories abound about where Jerome might have come from, none has ever been found to be grounded in anything that could be considered reliable evidence. Was he a mutinous pirate punished by having his legs expertly amputated or had he been the victim of an accident who was later disposed of when he became a burden? This is one of the few mysteries in this book that does not have anything closely resembling an answer or solution.

Many of the mysteries in this book are whodunnits, stories of murders that have gone unsolved or for which the wrong person might have been charged and convicted. There is no darker tale in Canada's history than that of the Black Donnellys, the family that was essentially slaughtered by their neighbours one evening. Apparently the Donnelly's litigious and confrontational ways caused great conflict in the community, and a vigilante group felt that the best way to deal with the family was to kill as many of them as possible. While some pretty good evidence exists as to who was responsible, and some individuals were brought to trial, no one was ever convicted for what was one of Canada's most notorious crimes.

There is the story of Tom Thomson, a gifted young painter whose associations and whose work helped create one of the most famous groups of painters Canada has ever known, and how he came to such an untimely and mysterious end. While some believe he was simply the victim of a boating accident, many others question the circumstances of his death and his burial. There is even witness testimony, collected decades after the fact, that Thomson might very well have been murdered by people he thought were his friends.

We know how Herbert Norman died—he chose to jump off a building in Egypt while he was serving as Canada's ambassador there. It is the reasons he chose to end his own life that are an enduring mystery to this day. Norman was dogged his entire professional life by allegations that he was a Communist, or that he had been. Yet if we look at the period and circumstances in which Norman grew up, we can see that there weren't too many intellectuals at the time who didn't, at one time or another in their lives, think that communism was an cure for the world's woes. More than the fact that he might have been a Communist, Norman was dogged by allegations that he was a spy. It was the Americans more than the Canadians who pursued a case against Norman. While his friend Lester Pearson was willing to keep defending him, Norman chose instead to take his own life at a time when he had accomplished the greatest achievement of his professional career as a diplomat. Did he kill himself to hide a secret, or because, as many believed, he just couldn't take it anymore?

And what of the Gerald Bull, the weapons designer who at one time was in the employ of one of the most hated men of the modern era, Saddam Hussein? The young engineer, known more for his work ethic and the force of his personality than for his intellectual prowess, became something of a phenom in the world of weapons and munitions. His goal was to develop a gun large enough to be able to shoot a satellite into orbit. He spent time in prison for smuggling arms to South Africa, designed weapons for China and, at the time of his death, was building two super guns in Iraq. Whether those guns were meant to launch satellites or to launch weapons has never been definitively proven. Nor has it been categorically demonstrated who, exactly, shot him five times in his Brussels apartment building. Maybe it was the Israelis, maybe the Iranians, maybe the Iraqis. It reads like, and has actually been used in, a spy thriller novel.

Granger Taylor just disappeared. The eccentric, young mechanical genius who had built his own vehicles and restored trains and bulldozers, one day, just disappeared seemingly off the face of the earth. He had been intrigued by the idea of UFOs and aliens, and had been telling people that aliens had even communicated with him telepathically. They were going to take him on an interstellar voyage lasting more than three years, so he left a note for his parents explaining where he was going, and he disappeared without a trace. While some evidence seems to indicate he died in either a terrible accident or by his own hand, some still believe that Granger is doing exactly what he said he was going to do.

No one knows who killed Peter Verigin, the leader of the Dukhobors, a group of communal-living pacifists who came to Canada from Russia to escape oppression. The Dukhobors succeeded in alienating and infuriating their neighbours, coming into conflict with provincial and federal governments and fighting within their community. Consequently, any one of these groups might have wanted Verigin dead, which they accomplished by blowing up a train in which he was riding. There are other theories though, including one that has nothing at all to do with Verigin.

William Robinson came to Salt Spring Island in the 1860s as an African American looking for freedom. What he got instead was a musket shot to the back that killed him inside his own home. A man from a local First Nations tribe was later tried, convicted and executed for Robinson's murder, yet within months of the hanging, another African American on the island was killed under similar circumstances, and no one was ever convicted in that murder. Was it really a murder by an Aboriginal person, or was it something more sinister, such as someone coveting Robinson's valuable land?

Sir Harry Oakes became Canada's richest man in the 1920s, but he fled the country for the Bahamas to escape excessive taxation and protect his wealth. He was murdered, and while his son-in-law was tried for killing Oakes, the son-in-law was acquitted when it was revealed that evidence had likely been fabricated. Various theories about who might have been responsible for Oakes' death range from American gangsters wanting to build casinos in the Bahamas to a former king of England trying to cover up a possibly sinister past.

And then there are Lyle and Marie McCann, a couple in their 70s from St. Albert, Alberta, who left the city in their motor home in July 2010 to meet up with their daughter in BC and never arrived. One man, Travis Vader, was taken into custody, held on other charges and eventually charged with the McCann's murder. Those charges were stayed, then brought back and finally a trial date was set for 2016. In between, it is alleged Vader has repeatedly broken the conditions of his bail, which he has claimed has been more a result of the RCMP trying to make his life miserable than of anything he has actually done wrong. This particular mystery was the most difficult to write, as I served as editor for the *St. Albert Gazette* when the McCanns disappeared. I see members of the family around the city from time to time, even today, and my heart goes out to them. What they've had to endure all of these years, has been

Interspersed among these detailed stories of mysterious circumstances and unexplained deaths are 10 condensed versions of well-known Canadian mysteries. People have been searching for the Lost Lemon Mine for many decades; even one of my own distant relations was one of the searchers. Sightings have been and are still being recorded of more than one ghost ship—the *Mary Celeste* and the ghost ship of Northumberland Strait. And what of the Beothuk, the Native tribe of the island of Newfoundland whose people have disappeared in the annals of time?

Over the years, there has been much theorizing and discussion about who really discovered Canada, both on the east coast and the west. Many historians believe they know, but what is the truth? Who made the first strike of the Klondike Gold Rush, who were the people that drew petroglyphs on the sandstone rocks in Saskatchewan, who was the Mad Trapper of Rat River and who *really* was the man behind the title *A Man Called Intrepid*? These are all mysteries some of which defy even our advanced technology today.

I think it's important, in all of the unsolved mysteries and crimes contained in this book, to remember that there were other victims in those stories, other than the people that died or disappeared. It feels like that fact is forgotten when people try to prove their conspiracy theory. I ask you, the reader, to keep this in mind as you read on.

Chapter 1

The Franklin Expedition

~

On Tuesday September 9, 2014, the national media based in Ottawa were called to a press conference at the Parks Canada headquarters. Prime Minister Stephen Harper was scheduled to attend.

Yet this was not a typical government press conference. No announcements were being made about funding for new projects or hiring new staff. This announcement had to do with history, and such announcements typically don't require the presence of the prime minister. In fact, few matters of Canadian history are so important that the prime minister needs to be involved, so this event caused more than a few whispers to circulate. The presence at the press conference of a tired-looking Ryan Harris, one of Parks Canada's underwater archaeologists, further fuelled those whispers.

The prime minister first spoke in French, which in hindsight was a strange choice considering the subject matter. But for those who weren't able to understand what he said in French, he quickly repeated the announcement in English.

"This is a day of some very good news, and that is that we have found one of the two Franklin ships," Harper said.

Before he could continue, the room broke out into wild applause, accompanied by hooting and hollering. The news was tremendous. After roughly 160 years of searching by various governments, research missions and private ventures, a department of the government of Canada had finally located one of the two ships that had been under the command of Captain John Franklin when he left England to try to find the Northwest Passage as a shortcut to the East.

Side-scan sonar of the first ship from Franklin's Lost Expedition. When this photo was taken it was unclear whether it was an image of the HMS *Erebus* or the HMS *Terror*.

After finishing his announcement, Harper and Harris rose and walked to another part of the room. Harper, with some help, removed a piece of fabric covering a large photo. It was a sonar image of the ship that had been found barely two days earlier somewhere in Canada's north. As the press looked on, Harris took over and began to explain to the assembled press corps what they were looking at. The ship was lying in approximately five metres of water off the bow and four metres off the stern. The sonar image was remarkably detailed. It showed that some of the deck structures, such as the mast, which had been sheared off, were still intact. Other items visible on the deck included the capstan (used to raise the anchor), the forward hatch and the forward pump head, as well as deck beams and diagonal deck planks that were known to be used by the Royal Navy on the two ships under Franklin's command—the HMS *Erebus* and HMS *Terror*. Harris told the press that the ship was "indisputably" one of Franklin's. He stated confidently that, given the well-preserved condition of the ship above decks, the parts of the ship below decks were also likely in as good condition.

But there were two questions no one could yet answer: Which of the two ships had they found? And where was the other one?

~

Commerce had driven much of the discovery of the New World. Christopher Columbus had been in search of the East Indies when he set sail, looking to reach Japan. Instead he reached the Bahamas archipelago. On his three subsequent voyages, he discovered the Americas. Jacques Cartier, who landed in Canada, had also been looking for some kind of western passage to Asia for the purpose of enhancing trade. By the 19th century it was becoming clear that, despite several attempts by various explorers, there was no shortcut through the Americas. Subsequent explorers had to either venture north or south to try to find a way to the Orient. Each attempt to reach Asia led to more mapping of the two continents, contributing to the greater overall knowledge of the area's geography. As such, many were convinced that a way to Asia could be found through Canada's north.

The British had already made several trips made into the area. Explorers such as Sir John Ross, Sir William Edward Parry and Sir James Clark Ross all probed the area with mixed success. They mapped some of the area but had not found a way through. As the middle of the 19th century approached, the part of Canada's north that was not mapped was an area of approximately 181,300 square kilometres. Undaunted, the British were convinced they could find a path through Canada's north to the Orient, and in 1845, commissioned a new expedition to further probe the area.

The expedition's first problem was finding someone to lead the expedition. Parry, an experienced Arctic explorer, was offered the command but declined, saying he was tired of the Arctic. Sir James Clark Ross was approached next, but he too turned it down, because he had promised his new wife he was done with Arctic exploration. A succession of alternate choices was rejected for various reasons: temperament, youth or

Sir John Franklin. Barrow reluctantly chose Sir John Franklin to lead the expedition.

nationality. Reluctantly, Sir John Barrow, Second Secretary of the Admiralty, selected Captain John Franklin to head up the two-ship mission.

Franklin was a veteran of Arctic exploration. He had served as second-in-command of a two-ship expedition to the North Pole in 1818. He had also commanded overland explorations along the Arctic coast from 1819–22 and 1825–27. When Barrow offered Franklin the command, he accepted. He was formally given the command on February 7, 1845.

The first problem facing the Franklin expedition was time. The ships on the mission needed to be laden down with as much preserved food as possible. A new way of preserving food, placing it in sealed tin cans, was available, but it wasn't until early April, only seven weeks before the expedition was to set sail, that Stephen Goldner received the contract to prepare a three-year food supply—8000 tins of food. The lack of time led to some careless work on Goldner's part. He used lead soldering to seal the tins, and much of the work was done sloppily. The food inside the tins was cooked inadequately, and the tins were not properly sealed thus allowing bacteria to enter and grow, therefore contaminating the food.

The two ships Franklin commanded were veterans of cold-weather exploration. The HMS *Erebus* and HMS *Terror* had been to the Antarctic with Sir James Clark Ross. The *Erebus,* the larger of the two ships at 343 tonnes, was Franklin's command ship, although James Fitzjames was in command of the actual ship. Francis Crozier was named executive officer of the expedition and commander of the 300-tonne HMS *Terror.* Both ships had steam engines that could propel them up to a maximum speed of 7.4 kilometres per hour (4 knots). The bows were reinforced with iron plating, and each actually had a steam-heating device to enhance crew comfort. The libraries aboard had as many as 1000 books to help keep the crew of 110 men and 24 officers occupied. Of the 134 men on board, only Franklin, Crozier, an assistant surgeon and two of the crew had any experience sailing in the Arctic.

The expedition left England on May 19, 1845. The ships made a stop in Scotland then sailed to Greenland with two other ships. In Greenland, the crew slaughtered 10 oxen for

Captain Francis Crozier, executive officer for the expedition, commanded HMS *Terror*.

~

fresh meat. The last letters from the crew were transferred to other ships for delivery to England. Five crewmembers were sent home before the ships left for Canada, leaving a total crew of 129. The last time any European saw either the *Erebus* or the *Terror*, was in July 1845 when the captains of the whaling ships *Prince of Wales* and *Enterprise* passed them in Baffin Bay. After that day, no European ever again laid eyes on the ships or any of the members of their crews.

It was not uncommon for explorations to take a long time—several months, sometimes even a year or more—and the expedition for all intents and purposes had a three-year supply of preserved food. So when 1845 passed into 1846 with no sightings or word from Franklin or the crew, little concern was raised. But that year passed, too, with no communication or sightings. By early 1848, the subject of the fate of the Franklin expedition was consuming much of Britain's population. That spring, the admiralty, facing pressure from Members of Parliament, the press and Franklin's wife, Lady Jane, finally launched a search mission for the presumed lost expedition. The search had three elements to it. One was an overland party that would launch down the Mackenzie River to the Arctic Coast of

Portrait of Jane Griffin (later Lady Franklin), 24, in 1815. She married John Franklin in 1828, a year before he was knighted.

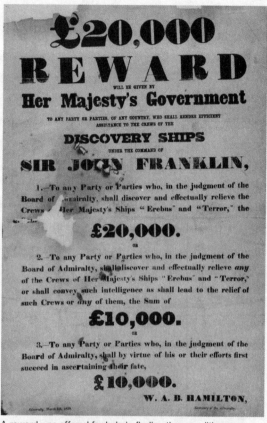

A reward was offered for help in finding the expedition.

~

Canada. Two other expeditions would also launch by sea. One would enter the north through Lancaster Sound, while the second would approach the north from the Pacific side. A reward of £20,000 was offered for locating or information that would lead to locating the expedition. Nothing was found. All three search parties returned with no information on the fate of Franklin's crew.

The failure of the search parties only added to the British public's growing concern. Starting in 1850, almost a dozen British ships, along with a pair of ships from the United States, scoured the known Arctic for traces of Franklin and his men. It was during these searches, however, that the first traces of the expedition were found. On Beechey Island, some of the search crews discovered the remains of a winter camp that would have been used by the crews. They also found three graves. The bodies inside were later identified as John Shaw Torrington, John Hartnell and William Braine, all preserved in remarkable condition as a result of the cold temperatures in the Arctic. But despite an intense search of the site, the searchers found no messages from the party.

Graves of the crewmen buried on Beechey Island

The ongoing search for Franklin consumed even more of Britain's ships. In 1852 Sir Edward Belcher was given command of five ships to explore the Arctic in search of Franklin and his crew. During the search, four of those ships were abandoned by the expedition because they were trapped in the ice.

News began to trickle in from other channels. Hudson's Bay Company employees were still scouring much of the colony that would become Canada. In 1854 an employee by the name of John Rae was surveying the Boothia Peninsula for the company when he met an Inuk man near present-day Kugarruk, Nunavut. In speaking with the man, Rae learned that the Inuit living in the area had seen a group of some 40 white men in the area. The men were seen dragging a boat and sledges with them. The sailors indicated through gestures that their ships had been crushed and they were heading south. They purchased a small seal or piece of seal meat from the Natives. The Inuk told Rae that all of the sailors had starved to death somewhere near the Back River.

Rae wrote:

April 1854. We were now joined by another one of the Natives who had been absent seal hunting yesterday, but being anxious to see us, visited our snow house early this morning, and then followed up our track. This man was very communicative, and on putting to him the usual questions as to having seen "white men" before or any ships or boats, he replied in the negative; but said, that a party of "Kabloonas" [white men; Europeans] *had died of starvation, a long distance to the west of where we then were,*

John Rae acquired the first Franklin expedition relics from the Inuit. He reported on starvation and cannibalism among the dying crewmen.

and beyond a large River. He stated that he did not know the exact place; that he had never been there and he could not accompany us so far.

As Rae spoke with other Inuit, he was able to confirm what he had learned to date both through the stories the Inuit told and through some of items the Inuit had in their possession. They had several pieces of silvery cutlery that were later identified as belonging to the expedition. Rae also learned one hair-raising detail that would later prove to be extremely controversial back in England. The Inuit said that some of the men they had encountered had resorted to cannibalism in a last desperate attempt to survive.

"From the mutilated state of many of the bodies and the contents of the kettles, it is evident that our wretched country-men had been driven to the last dread alternative—cannibalism—as a means of prolonging existence," Rae wrote.

When Rae's report about the fate of the Franklin expedition reached London, its contents, specifically the suggestion that the sailors had resorted to cannibalism, horrified and repulsed the British public, and many outright denied the possibility. No one could envision any proper member of the Royal Navy engaging in the practice, no matter how desperate they might have been. As a result, Rae's character was attacked for reporting that information.

No less than the famous author Charles Dickens launched a campaign to discredit Rae and what he had reported. Specifically, Dickens suggested that the Inuit, which he referred to as "Esquimaux," had probably murdered the members of the Franklin expedition, saying they were "a gross handful of uncivilised people with a domesticity of blood and blubber." As a result of the controversy, although he spent much of his life surveying the Arctic and was credited by some with more of the discovery of the Northwest Passage than Franklin, Rae was refused a knighthood while Franklin was posthumously promoted to Rear Admiral of the Blue.

When the Admiralty received the report, it asked the Hudson's Bay Company if it could send some people down the Back River in the hopes of finding either more signs of the expedition or any of the actual crew. Those searches led to the finding of more artifacts and more stories from the Inuit about groups of white men starving to death. Among the more telling finds was a piece of wood with the word "Erebus" on it and a second piece of wood that bore the name of the surgeon posted aboard HMS *Erebus*. Based on this new information, as well as that received earlier, along with the fact 10 years had passed without any sign of the expedition, the Admiralty officially declared Franklin and his crew dead in May 1854.

But Jane Franklin refused to believe that her husband was dead and, using her own funds, she personally commissioned one more search party. Sir Francis Leopold McClintock led the expedition that left in July 1857. The crew set sail on board the steam schooner *Fox*, complete with teams of sled dogs, in search of Franklin and his men. From the beginning of the trip, McClintock scoured the north but came away with little more evidence of the whereabouts of the Franklin crew. Search parties using the sled dogs did come into contact with large groups of Inuit, from whom McClintock's men took testimony. Some of those Inuit described seeing a three-masted ship crushed by the ice somewhere west of King William Island. Other groups of Inuit described seeing two ships near the island, one of which sank while the second was smashed by the ice. The Inuit also said there was a body aboard the second ship. Many of these Inuit had in their possession relics belonging to the Franklin expedition, and McClintock purchased all he came across from them.

McClintock's Arctic expedition in search of Franklin at Meville Bay; sketch of *Resolute*, caught in the ice; *Intrepid*; *North Star*; and a whaler.

Finally, in April 1859, a party that had gone ashore at King William Island came across the first real sign of what had happened to the crew. The men found a stone cairn that contained a piece of paper. On that one piece of paper were written two different notes. The first note, dated May 28, 1847, read:

H.M. ships Erebus *and* Terror *wintered in the ice in 28 of May, 1847 at lat. 70* 5' N. long 98* 23' W. Having wintered in 1846–7 at Beechey Island in lat. 74* 43' 28" N.; long. 91* 39' 15" W. after having ascended Wellington Channel to lat. 77* and returned by the west side of Cornwallis Island.*

Sir John Franklin commanding the expedition.

All Well.

Party consisting of 2 officers and 6 men left the ships on Monday 24 May 1847.

Gm. Gore, Lieut.

Chas. F. Des Voeus, Mate.

The second note, written in the margins of the first, was dated April 25, 1848, not quite a year after the date of the first note. This message was much more grim.

H.M. ships Terror *and* Erebus *were deserted on the 22d April, 5 leagues N. N. W. of this, having been beset since 12th September 1846. The officers and crews, consisting of 105 souls, under the command of Captain F.R.M Crozier, landed here in lat. 69* 37" 42" N., long. 98* 41' W. Sir John Franklin died on the 11th June 1847; and the total loss by deaths in the expedition has been to this date 9 officers and 15 men.*

The letter went on to say, "and start (on) to-morrow 26th, for Back's Fish River."

Both notes have been subject to intense scrutiny by scholars and amateur Franklin detectives over the years, and several discrepancies have been pointed out. The first note, which seems to depict that all is well on the expedition, likely has an incorrect date. A reconstruction of the expedition's probable timeline shows that they most likely wintered on Beechey Island during 1845–46, but the date on the note is one year later. The second issue with the note is signature. Despite the assertion in the note that everything is fine, analysis of the handwriting in the note shows that it was written, not by

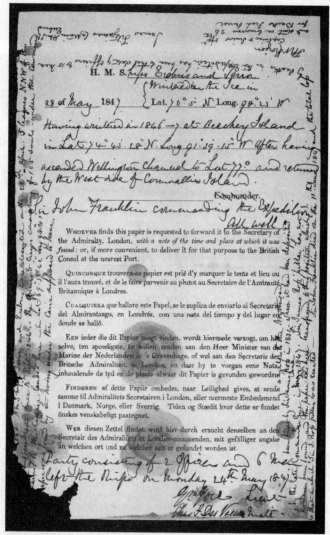

Note found by Francis Leopold McClintock's Expedition team in a cairn on King William Island in 1859. The notes detail the fate of the Franklin Expedition. Written on a standard Admiralty form, two messages are visible.

Franklin but by James Fitzjames, commander of HMS *Erebus*. It was standard practice for the expedition commander to write such notes.

An answer to why Franklin didn't write the note himself might lie in the date of his death given in the second note. According to the author of that note, Franklin died on June 11, 1847, approximately three weeks after the date of the first note. Scholars have suggested that the reason Fitzjames wrote the note is that Franklin may have been incapacitated by whatever it was that led to his death. In addition, the second note gives no information at all about the cause of Franklin's death or where his body might have been buried.

Another question raised by the second note comes from the casualty figures given. According to the note, at the time of its writing, 9 officers and 15 crew had died. When one compares those fatalities to the ships complement when it left Greenland of 24 officers and 109 men, it shows that a significantly higher percentage of officers died than did enlisted crew—37 percent of the officers had perished, compared to 14 percent of the crew. The note makes no mention of what exactly befell the party to create such a strange discrepancy in casualties among the expedition's officers and crew.

The last line too has confused scholars. In it, the author of the note—believed to be the expedition's executive officer and captain of HMS *Terror* Francis Crozier—says that a party was leaving for Back's Fish River. What is not known is exactly who left for Back's Fish River. Was it the entire remaining expedition complement, or was it a small search party? What was the

A sledge encampment during Sir Francis McClintock's search for Franklin, sketched by Admiral Sir Leopold McClinktock. The camp was located south of Cornwallis Island.

purpose of their trip to the Back's Fish River, which was known to be a challenging river to portage? Were they hoping to find a group of Inuit to trade with or to seek help from, or were they trying to get closer to Repulse Bay in the hopes of catching the attention of a passing ship?

McClintock's expedition yielded many more finds. His crew found a human skeleton with the papers for a Chief Petty Officer Peglar, who had served aboard HMS *Terror*. It was later determined, because the body was dressed in a uniform belonging to a different member of the crew, that the papers had been placed with the body. His crew also came across a lifeboat and two skeletons on King William Island. The lifeboat was filled abandoned equipment such as boots, handkerchiefs, soap, slippers, combs and books. Continued exploration also uncovered a second stone cairn with a second note, this one left by Lieutenant Gore in May 1847. Its contents were similar to the first note found. In August 1859, McClintock and his crew began the journey back to England, making port in London on September 21.

McClintock's expedition was not the only one to come across relics from Franklin's expedition in the area. Charles Francis Hall, who lived among the Inuit in the area of Frobisher Bay on Baffin Island, led two expeditions. One trip took place in 1860 and one in 1869. He came across camps, relics and graves, but found no sign that any members of the expedition might be living among the Inuit. In his travels, Hall collected hundreds of pages of testimony from the Inuit he encountered. That testimony included stories of encountering a group of white men on the southern part of King William Island.

Charles Francis Hall

While a few other expeditions set out in the years following Hall's journey, little else of any value was discovered, and interest in discovering the fate of Franklin and his men began to wane. In England, Franklin was celebrated as a hero and was even credited, though no evidence existence that he had actually found it, with discovering the Northwest Passage. A statue of Franklin was erected in his hometown of Spilsby, Lincolnshire, England, with the inscription "John Franklin—Discoverer of the Northwest Passage." Other statues in Franklin's honour were erected outside the Athenaeum in London and in Tasmania. Other than these monuments, for the most part, Franklin and his men were lost to history.

The search for answers to what happened to Franklin and his men didn't resume until 1981 when Owen Beattie, a professor of anthropology at the University of Alberta in Edmonton, decided it was time to further investigate the fate of the Franklin expedition. In June 1981 Beattie and a team of researchers travelled to King William Island. Their goal was to use modern forensic science to identify the human remains in the area and try to determine cause of death. The team retraced the steps of some of the explorers that had looked for Franklin in the 19th century. Despite an extensive search, the team uncovered only a few samples of human remains. A closer look at the remains unveiled some pitting and scaling in the bones that was known to occur in individuals suffering from scurvy, a condition brought on by a vitamin C deficiency. Closer inspection also turned up marks on some of the bones that Beattie felt was consistent with cannibalism.

When their mission was finished, Beattie and his team returned to Edmonton and sent some of the collected bone samples to the Alberta Soil and Feed Testing laboratory to see what trace elements might be present in the bones. The results shocked Beattie. The bones that were believed to belong to members of the Franklin expedition showed a lead content of 226 parts per million. In comparison, samples from Inuit remains that were taken as control samples had a lead content of only 26-36 parts per million. Beattie returned to the Arctic the following summer and scoured the west coast of King William Island. This search was much more fruitful; they came across the remains of between 6 to 14 people, as well as a few other relics.

Still, the lead findings were intriguing, especially given that it was known even then that lead was a highly toxic chemical. In earlier times, lead was used in house paint, as well as in metal typesetting, plumbing and shotgun pellets. It was also used as a soldering agent. It was known that exposure to lead could cause numerous health problems, including pain, weakness in the fingers, wrists and ankles and fertility issues in men. Lead poisoning has been shown to damage nerve connections and cause other brain and blood disorders. It can also cause problems with mental functioning, including memory loss and mood disorders. That information, coupled with the discovery of the high lead content in the bone samples, gave Beattie an idea. Could the men of the Franklin expedition have been suffering from lead poisoning? Could lead poisoning have contributed to, even intensified, the scurvy the men were suffering from, to the point that the scurvy had become lethal?

Beattie had many potential sources of lead to consider. The pewter tableware, lead-wicked candles, food colouring and tobacco products, as well as tins of food products lined with lead foil and the lead solder used on the tin cans likely contaminated all the food with lead. Beattie, however, wanted to test some soft tissue, as bone concentrations of lead could have reflected lifetime lead exposure instead of just the exposure the men suffered on their last voyage. Beattie and his team travelled to Beechey Island, a known location of casualties' graves of the Franklin expedition. The team exhumed and examined the body of John Torrington. They quickly examined the body of John Hartnell but were forced to abandon their research because of bad weather conditions. They did, however, return to Edmonton with samples of Torrington's hair and bones. As a result of their analysis, they were able to conclude that Torrington had suffered "severe mental and physical problems" as a result of lead poisoning. Torrington's actual cause of death was determined to be pneumonia, but lead poisoning was listed as having contributed to his demise. A photo of Torrington, his body incredibly well preserved as a result of being buried in the Arctic, was released to the public and helped galvanize public attention once again on what happened to the Franklin expedition.

The team came across fragments from dozens of food tins that had been thrown away by the crew of the expedition. In his examination of the tins, Beattie noted that the seams of the tin cans had been soldered poorly and that lead had been used to seal the tins. This could have been the source of the acute lead poisoning found in the bones of the remains. Others disagreed. Some researchers instead pointed to a water distillation system that was fitted into both ships. Some of the materials that were used at the time to build the distillation system could have leeched lead into the water, which could also explain the high levels of lead that Beattie had found.

Beattie's expeditions led to a resurgence in the search for relics of the expedition and for the lost ships. One search in 1992 uncovered 400 bones and bone fragments, as well as relics such as clay pipes and brass fittings. This same expedition found marks on other bones to further prove that some of the men had resorted to cannibalism in an effort to survive.

Another search in 1992 tried to find what had happened to the two ships *Terror* and *Erebus*, and even enlisted help from the Canadian Forces to identify several areas of the Arctic Ocean with strong magnetic readings. Despite using sonar to display an image of the sea bottom in those areas where the magnetic readings could have come from a ship, no evidence of either of the two ships was ever found. From 1995 on, several other expeditions scoured various parts of the Arctic, but besides finding a few relics, no great discoveries and no traces of either ship were located.

In 2008 the Canadian government announced it was ramping up its efforts to find HMS *Terror* and HMS *Erebus*. The effort was not simply a historical exercise; it was hoped that finding the ships would lend more legitimacy to Canada's claims over large areas of the Arctic. Parks Canada led a search that began in August 2008 in the waters off King William Island.

The expedition also had the fortune of being able to draw on a new book that had been published containing details from the Inuit that hadn't previously been reported. Those reports stated that some Inuit had a seen a ship anchored off the Royal Geographical Society Islands in the winter of 1850. Armed with that information, as well as noted underwater archaeologist Robert Grenier, the crews set out for the first six-week search in what was to be a three-year project.

"I cannot promise to find the ship. But we have a decent chance," Grenier said. He had earlier described the two ships as the Holy Grail of North American shipwrecks.

Unfortunately, that first expedition yielded little more than a few bits of metal and nails that may have come from one the ships. The searchers carried on, but other news emerged from relics found during the expedition. A test by researchers from McMaster University and the Royal Ontario Museum discovered that the lead content of a 160-year-old can of ox-cheek soup was "off the scale." The finding added more fuel to the theory that the lead soldering of the cans may have caused lead poisoning in the crew.

In July 2010, a spokesperson for the crew made a huge announcement. The search crews hadn't found *Terror* or *Erebus*, but they had found the next best thing—the HMS *Investigator*, a ship that had sailed from England in 1850 as part of the search for the Franklin expedition. The ship had quickly become trapped in ice, and its 69-member crew had sought shelter in Mercy Bay, spending two winters there. The crew divided itself into three parties. Two parties went overland in search of help while the third stayed with the ship, hoping the ice would melt in the coming summer. A crewmember from one of the overland expeditions returned to the *Investigator* to report he had found two other ships nearby, both of which were much better equipped, but also trapped in the ice. The crew of *Investigator* abandoned ship and set off, eventually finding HMS *Resolute*. They spent a fourth winter in the ice before eventually leaving the Arctic aboard HMS *Northern Star* and returning to England. Captain Robert McClure, the commander of *Investigator*, was later given a £10,000 reward for discovering the Northwest Passage. His ship had never been found because of terrible weather and sea ice in the area, but for nearby Inuit, it proved to be a boon. The Inuit salvaged the copper in the siding of ship and used it extensively. As a result, the Inuit of the region were subsequently referred to as the Copper Inuit.

Finally when the ship was found in 2010, the *Investigator* was upright in shallow water. The *Investigator's* decks were only eight metres below the surface of the water. The searchers also found three graves nearby. While the *Investigator* was a historic find of great importance, crews were still feverishly searching for HMS *Terror* and HMS *Erebus*.

New searches in 2011, 2012 and 2013 revealed nothing, despite extensive searches of the Victoria Strait/Alexandra Strait region and the southern region of O'Reilly Island. New human remains were found at Erebus Bay, where up to a dozen crewmembers were known to have died. But no sign of either ship emerged, despite the use of military-grade side-scan sonar and unmanned underwater vehicles.

In 2014, Parks Canada led a four-vessel flotilla into the north. The crews were supposed to be heading for the Victoria Strait, but it was so covered in ice that they chose instead to search further south around Queen Maud Gulf. On September 1, two archaeologists from the Government of Nunavut took a chopper ride to Hat Island to mark the location of some early Inuit tent sites when they spotted two objects below. Those two objects turned out to be crucial finds. The first was an iron fitting that turned out to be a boat-launching davit. The davit bore the stamp of the Royal Navy. The second find was a wooden plug for a deck hawse (the iron pipe through which the ship's chain cable would have been lowered into the chain locker). Not only were these the first significant artifacts found in modern times, but their location acted as an enormous arrow for crews searching for the shipwrecks.

On September 7, Parks Canada archaeologists Jonathan Moore and Ryan Harris were on duty, monitoring the sonar as their ship trolled the waters of the eastern part of Queen Maud Gulf when they saw the unmistakable outline of a ship. The archaeologists superimposed a drawing of the ship over the sonar image. It was a match to the HMS *Erebus*. The excitement that followed was palpable. Archaeologists Ryan Harris and Jonathan Moore later likened it to "winning the Stanley Cup." The following day, they brought in a remotely operated submersible into the area to confirm their find. The scientists immediately flew to Ottawa so they could be present for the announcement. Prime Minister Stephen Harper announced to Canada and the world that one of the wrecks had been found. The Canadian Government immediately notified the government of England, since the Franklin expedition had sailed from that country. England replied with a message from none other than Queen Elizabeth herself.

"I was greatly interested to learn of the discovery of one of the long-lost ships of Captain Sir John Franklin," the Queen said in her statement. "Prince Philip joins me in sending congratulations and good wishes to all those who played a part in this historic achievement."

The location of the ship was at first kept secret from the public, to dissuade pleasure seekers and treasure hunters from disturbing the find. That the crews had even been looking in what was later revealed to be the eastern Queen Maud Gulf was something of a stroke of luck. The crews had been planning to search a different stretch of water but had been forced towards the eastern Queen Maud Gulf by the thick ice.

The only question left to answer was which of the two ships had been located. That answer came less than a month later, and it was again Prime Minister Harper who informed the world. Harper rose in the House of Commons to make the announcement.

"I'm delighted to confirm that we have identified which ship from the Franklin expedition has been found," Harper said. "It is, in fact, the HMS *Erebus*."

HMS *Erebus* was the ship historians were most hopeful to find, because it served as Franklin's flagship for the expedition. Not only would it mean that many of his personal papers and the expeditions logs might still be aboard, but they speculated that Franklin himself may have died aboard the ship, so it may have served as Franklin's final resting place.

"Franklin was based aboard *Erebus*, that ship is where he lived and likely where he died. It was at the very centre of this great historical mystery. The stunning condition of the ship and the artifacts represent a global treasure," said John Geiger, CEO of the Royal Canadian Geographical Society.

Yet how those artifacts might be recovered and explored is as of this writing unknown. The government has made it clear that it is highly unlikely it will try to raise the ship. Not only would doing so be difficult and expensive, but the ship is potentially an underwater grave for some of Franklin's men, perhaps even Franklin himself. Government archaeologists subsequently believe that the site must be protected.

But that won't stop archaeologists from trying to bring up some of the artifacts aboard the ship. In November, a bell that was recovered from *Erebus* was unveiled to the public. It was revealed that a team of underwater archaeologists had recovered the bell from the deck of the ship near its windlass, a kind of anchor winch. Records show the bell was originally hung in that location. Aside from some corrosion from spending almost 170 years underwater, the bell was shown to be in excellent condition. Clearly visible was the engraving of "1845," the year the bell was cast, as was the embossed broad arrow, identifying it as the property of the British government.

The whereabouts of HMS *Terror* are still not known. The search continues, but artifacts from *Erebus* have been brought to the surface. To date several have been recovered, including buttons, ceramic plates, a cannon and most importantly, the ship's bronze bell. Many of these artifacts have been put on display in Gatineau, Québec.

Mary Celeste Ghost Ship

~

Initially christened as the *Amazon*, the *Mary Celeste* was a merchant ship originally built in Nova Scotia. Her keel was laid in 1860, and she was launched in 1861. She sailed cargo across the Atlantic until 1867 when she was driven ashore in a storm at Cape Breton Island and abandoned. An American mariner purchased her; he restored the ship and changed her name to *Mary Celeste*.

In November 1872, the *Mary Celeste* left port in New York for Genoa with a cargo of 1701 barrels of denatured alcohol. On December 4, the crew of the *Dei Gratia*, a Canadian ship, spotted the *Mary Celeste* between the Azores and the coast of Portugal. There was no one on deck, and no one replied to signals from the *Dei Gratia*. A boarding party found the ship deserted, its only lifeboat missing. The last entry in the *Mary Celeste's* log was dated November 25, but it did not indicate anything was wrong. Besides a few missing papers and some water in the hold, there were no signs of any crisis or violence. The *Dei Gratia* towed the *Mary Celeste* to Gibraltar.

A salvage hearing noted some strange finds, such as cuts on each side of bow, apparent blood on the captain's sword and stains on the ship's rails that may have also been blood. The final report was fantastical, indicating the crew had gotten into the alcohol and in a drunken orgy, murdered the captain and his family, cut the bow to simulate a collision and fled in the lifeboat.

Other theories as to what might have happened include an attempt at insurance fraud, an attack by pirates, encountering a dangerous waterspout or an iceberg. Another theory cites the release of fumes from the alcohol and potential for explosion that could have led the crew to abandon the ship. The captain and her crew were never seen or heard from again.

Chapter 2

Tom Thomson

~

No examination of the great mysteries and unexplained of Canada would be complete without touching on the mysterious circumstances surrounding the death and subsequent disposal of the remains of one Canada's great artists and forerunner to the group that would eventually call themselves the Group of Seven, Tom Thomson.

Mystery and confusion have surrounded Thomson's death since the day in 1917 when he disappeared. Little more light was shed on the circumstances of his demise when his body was found several days later, and the way in which is body was handled led to much speculation and conjecture about where Thomson might actually be buried. Just as many theories exist about exactly how Thomson died. As this chapter will seek to demonstrate, while modern science may have given Canadians a better idea of where Thomson was laid to rest, the exact cause of his death is still in dispute.

~

It took Thomson quite some time to establish himself as an artist. He was born near Claremont, Ontario, to John and Margaret Thomson on August 5, 1877. Thomson was one of nine children in the family, and he had four older brothers. While he was born in Claremont, the family moved to Leith, near Owen Sound, where Thomson grew up. It took him some time once he reached adulthood to find his direction in life. In 1899 he a close family friend granted him a machine shop apprenticeship position at his iron foundry. Unfortunately, Thomson habitually showed up late for work, and it was for this reason he was eventually fired from the foundry. Soon after he was fired, he tried to enlist in the military to fight in the Boer War, a conflict that saw Canada dispatch troops overseas for the first time. Some 7000 Canadians fought in the war in South Africa, but Thomson was rejected from service because of a medical condition.

Tom Thomson, member of the Group of Seven

He found work for a time as a fire ranger in Algonquin Park, an area of Ontario that would have a profound influence on his later artistic work, and featured prominently in his disappearance and death. In 1901, Thomson decided to enrol in a business college in Chatham, Ontario, but dropped out after eight months. Instead he headed to Seattle, Washington, where he helped George, one of his older brothers, run a business school. He returned to Canada three years later, and he began to find an increasing amount of work using his budding artistic skills. He also started taking painting lessons. He found work in 1907 with an artistic design firm in Toronto named Grip Ltd., where he worked as a letterer, someone who inserted actual text into images. Also employed at Grip were several individuals who would later form the renowned Group of Seven.

But the Group of Seven was still several years away from actually forming, and as Thomson's artistic skills improved, he started dedicating himself more and more to his painting. In 1912 he moved on to Rous and Mann Press but quit the following year so he could dedicate himself full-time to his work. The Government of Ontario purchased one of his works in 1913, *The Northern Lake*, for $250, a tidy sum in that day and age. That same year Thomson had his first exhibit with the Ontario Society of Artists. He became an official member in 1914 when the National Gallery of Canada purchased one of his paintings. He shared both living and studio space with other artists.

For his inspiration, Thomson was drawn to the natural beauty of Algonquin Park, the oldest provincial park in Canada. He was familiar with the area, having worked as a fire ranger

The Jack Pine by Tom Thomson, 1916–17

and even part-time as a guide in the area. He was especially drawn to Canoe Lake. He began spending the majority of his summers out in the park, often staying at the Mowat Lodge, which was owned by a Shannon and Annie Fraser. While he was in the park, Thomson devoted himself to the artistic process. He carried small rectangles of paper with him to capture images that caught his attention and inspired him. He produced oil sketches on these smaller panels, generating hundreds of them between 1912 and 1917. He then worked on creating paintings based on those sketches. When summer was over, Thomson returned to Toronto where he spent his time alternating between painting and working on commercial contracts to help pay the rent. Thomson also had the financial assistance of a patron in James MacCallum, a Toronto-based doctor. Thomson's actual studio in Toronto was an old utility shack on the grounds of the Studio Building in Rosedale, it's only real amenity a wood-burning stove to help beat back the cold. According to those who study art, Thomson's style resembled that of Post-Impressionists such as Vincent Van Gogh and Paul Cézanne. His paintings seemed to convey a great respect for the natural environment from which he drew his inspiration, untouched by the progress of mankind.

Thomson's cabin, originally located on Severn Street in Toronto behind the Studio Building. It was moved in 1962 to be part of the McMichael Canadian Art Collection.

It was during his summers on Canoe Lake that Thomson met and became romantically involved with a woman who frequented the area. Winnifred Trainor was one of two daughters of Hugh and Margaret Trainor, who owned a cabin in the park. It was here in 1913 that Winnifred, often called Winnie, met Thomson and the two formed a relationship. Many different narratives are told of this relationship. Some convey it as a happy union, with the two engaged to be married and actively planning their honeymoon. Others portray Thomson as a reluctant suitor who didn't feel compelled to settle down with Winnie.

In the summer of 1917, Thomson was back at Canoe Lake, looking for and sketching the environment around him. He was starting to become well known as an artist. The National Gallery of Canada purchased the painting *Northern River* for $500. On the evening of July 7, 1917, Thomson attended a party at the cabin of a man named George Rowe. While he was at the party, Thomson ended up in a heated argument with one of the guests, Martin Blecher Jr., who has been erroneously portrayed in some accounts of Thomson's death as an American draft dodger. Some of the other guests at the party intervened in the argument, and Thomson subsequently left. In most accounts of his story, this was the last time anyone saw Thomson alive.

The next day, July 8, Thomson set off in his canoe on Canoe Lake. It was one of his favourite pastimes, and he was a skilled canoeist. On July 9, a canoe was found upside down on the lake. The canoe was empty, with the exception of some equipment that had been tied down to its interior. The canoe was instantly recognized as Thomson's, as he had apparently used a specific paint mixture for the colour of his canoe—a mix of grey and blue. Word that Thomson's canoe had been found upside down, with no sign of Thomson, quickly circulated throughout the surrounding area. By the following day, members of the community began searching the area for signs of Thomson. On July 12, the Frasers, who ran Mowat Lodge, where Thomson stayed in the summer, sent a telegram to Thomson's family letting them know that Thomson's canoe had been found and that the artist was missing. The park ranger, Mark Robinson, began hiking trails throughout the park that Thomson was known to frequent. Robinson found no trace of Thomson.

Tom's older brother George showed up at Canoe Lake in response to the telegram sent by the Frasers. Yet within two days, George left the lake, taking with him all of Tom's sketches and paintings. People continued to search for Thomson, but no one could find any trace of where he could be or what could have happened to him.

On July 16 at approximately 10:00 AM, one of the guests in the area, Dr. Goldwin Howland, a neurologist from the University of Toronto, was standing on the front steps of his cabin near the lake when he spotted something that seemed out of place on the surface of Canoe Lake. He hollered to a group that was canoeing nearby and asked them to go and check it out. That group paddled over and quickly identified the object as a human body. The undertaker was called, and the body was retrieved from the lake. The body, in an advanced state of decay after days spent in the water, was quickly identified as that of Tom Thomson.

The examination of any person that has died under unusual circumstances typically fell to the coroner of the region. A telegram was sent, requesting the coroner come to Canoe Lake to inspect Thomson's body. However, Dr. Howland, the neurologist who spotted the body in the lake, took it upon himself to examine the body. The corpse was bloated from having spent approximately eight days in the water, was starting to decay and had suffered damage from the elements. Upon closer inspection, Howland found a length of fishing line tied around Thomson's left ankle. The fishing line was tightly wrapped around the ankle 16 or 17 times. Further inspection of the body revealed an injury to Thomson's right temple, approximately 10 centimetres long. Some reports have indicated that some blood was found in one of Thomson's ears. Even though there was no evidence of any internal examination having taken place, Howland stated that the cause of Thomson's death was drowning.

Here is how Howland described his findings in his subsequent report:

> *Body of Tom Thomson, artist, found floating in Canoe Lake, July 16, 1917. Certified to be the person named by Mark Robinson, Park Ranger. Body clothed in grey lumberman's shirt, khaki trousers and canvas shoes. Head shows marked swelling of face, decomposition has set in, air issuing from mouth. Head has a bruise over left temple as if produced by falling on rock. Examination of body*

shows no bruises, body greatly swollen, blisters on limbs,
putrefaction setting in on surface. There are no signs of any
external force having caused death, and there is no doubt
but that death occurred from drowning.

Robinson gave an account to an author for a book about
Thomson that closely resembled what Howland had written in
his report:

I assisted Roy Dixon undertaker of Sprucedale, Ontario, to
take the body from the water in the presence of Dr. How-
land there were no marks on the body except a slight bruise
over the left eye. His fishing line was wound several times
around his left ankle and broken off. There was no sign
of the rod his Provisions and kit bag were in the front
end of the Canoe when found. The lake was not Rough.

What happened next is critical to the enduring mystery
over where Thomson's remains are located. For reasons that were
never adequately explained and that seem confounding to many
who know the story, the rather rash decision was made by all
those involved at the lake to bury Thomson there. Immediately.
The request was sent to the park superintendent, who approved
it. Thomson's body was placed in a wooden casket and buried in
a deep hole in the earth at Mowat Cemetery. At this time, the
story goes that Winnie Trainor came forward and demanded to
see Thomson's remains, but her request was not granted. Martin
Blecher Senior directed a small ceremony held at the gravesite
at Mowat Cemetery. Mr. Blecher was believed to be the father of
the man that Thomson had argued with the night before he
disappeared.

Winnie Trainor, meanwhile, had been in touch with the Thomson family. She sent them a telegram detailing what had taken place to date. In the subsequent telegrams exchanged, it was agreed that the Thomson family would send an undertaker on the next available train to Canoe Lake to exhume Thomson's remains and take them by train to Leith. Once in Leith, Thomson would be interred in the family plot at Leith Presbyterian Church. In the interim, another strange incident occurred that has only helped deepen the mystery around the circumstances of Thomson's death. The coroner, Dr. Arthur Ranney, arrived to conduct an autopsy. However, Ranney did nothing of the kind. He did not examine the body. He merely agreed with Dr. Howland's conclusion that the cause of Thomson's death was drowning, and he left.

On July 18, the undertaker sent by the Thomson family arrived. He brought with him a steel casket to transport Thomson's remains. The undertaker's name was F.W. Churchill. Upon being showing where Thomson was buried, Churchill told everyone he would like to get to work. He insisted on working alone, so everyone left. But after only approximately three hours, Churchill emerged from the place he had been working, telling everyone that he was finished. This seemed suspicious to many of the lake's residents. In that span of three hours, Churchill would have had to single-handedly dig down into the earth several feet using only a shovel, somehow extract Thomson's wooden coffin from the grave, transfer the corpse to the new steel casket, and then fill the grave back in. Mark Robinson, the ranger, was particularly suspicious that Churchill had accomplished all of that in the three-hour window, but Robinson apparently didn't challenge Churchill when he left with the casket to catch the next train. Porters who helped load the casket onto the train apparently later commented that the coffin did seem much lighter than they were expecting.

So there you have it. The only real element of this story that seems to be beyond dispute is that Tom Thomson died, and his body was found in a lake. Neither the cause of his death nor exactly what happened to his remains has ever been definitively proven.

The conduct and haste with which the undertaker apparently worked created some doubt as to whether or not he had actually taken Thomson's remains with him when he left Canoe Lake. Those mutterings persisted for years until one woman decided it was time to start trying to put together the true story of what had happened to Thomson. In 1935, Blowden Davies published a book about Thomson's death, entitled *A Study of Tom Thomson: The Story of a Man Who Looked for Beauty and for Truth in the Wilderness*. Davies, a journalist by training, self-published 500 copies of the book, which was one of the first major written works to cast doubt on the official narrative of Thomson's death. The book was subsequently edited and republished in 1967. She conducted interviews with people who had knowledge of the circumstances of Thomson's death. One of those people was Mark Robinson, the ranger at Algonquin Park.

A quote from Robinson seems to sum up that a great deal of skepticism existed as to what had happened to Thomson.

> *We buried his remains in the little cemetery at Canoe Lake, Martin Blecher Sr. reading the Anglican funeral service at the grave. Later his remains were taken up and went to Owen Sound for burial. Dr. Ranney of North Bay conducted what inquest was held. Tom was said to have been drowned. It may be quite true but the mystery remains.*

Yet despite the questions raised by the book as to the location of Thomson's body, the issue was never settled and seemed to fade into history. But in 1956, a small episode of drunken grave robbing reignited the entire debate about Thomson's burial place. One evening, a family court judge named William T. Little was drinking with a group of three friends when they got the tremendous idea to dig up the grave in the park that was believed to be where Thomson was originally buried. The skeleton they uncovered only created more confusion. On the skeleton's left temple, where Dr. Howland had, in his report on the body, noted the presence of a bruise on the head, there was actually a hole the size of a bullet.

Ignoring, for the moment, the fact a sitting judge decided to partake in an evening of drunken vandalism, for which he was apparently never punished, the find raised even more questions. One member of the group had the forethought to snap a quick photo of the skull, apparently for the sake of posterity.

The bones were supposedly then sent off for forensic examination. Any hope Little and his friends had that an examination
of their find would answer the enduring question of where
Thomson was buried were dashed when a representative of
the Government of Ontario reported that the bones belonged to
a 22-year-old Aboriginal male. The hole in the temple, the government said, was the result of a procedure known as trephination, where a hole is drilled into the skull to relieve pressure on
the brain. Little and his friends didn't believe that account, but
they had nothing further to use to make an argument. The
Thomson family refused to allow the remains supposedly buried
at Leith to be exhumed so they could be verified as Thomson's.
Eventually, in 1970, Little decided to use the information he
discovered to write a book entitled *The Tom Thomson Mystery*.

The picture of the skull, though, would prove instrumental in making the most compelling case yet for the location
of Thomson's remains. The photo eventually came into the possession of Roy MacGregor, a Canadian author and journalist.
MacGregor had actually grown up near where Winnie Trainor
lived and had known the woman in his youth. He had even
written one book of fiction based on Thomson's story. However,
with the picture of the skull found by Little in his hands, Mac-
Gregor set about trying to prove who was—or wasn't—buried
in the grave near Canoe Lake.

MacGregor tried to use modern forensic science to prove
his theory, that Tom Thomson's body never left Canoe Lake.
He had help from Ron Williamson, an adjunct professor of

archaeology at the University of Toronto. Williamson ran a business called Archaeological Services, which specialized in investigating exhumed human remains. Close inspection of the picture of the skull by Archaeological Services led to the conclusion that the skull belonged to someone of European ancestry, not to an Aboriginal male. Susan Pfeiffer, an internationally recognized forensic analysis expert who examined the skull, declared that it belonged to a middle-aged, Caucasian man.

The experts also took on the hole in the temple and the explanation provided in the 1950s, that it was the result of the procedure known as trephination. They observed that it would have been unwise to make such a hole in the temple for the procedure because the bone in the temple is thicker than in other parts of the skull. A computer program was brought into play as well to map the physical features of the skull and match them against the features of Thomson's actual face. As MacGregor quoted those experts in an essay for *The Globe and Mail*, "there is no morphological characteristic that suggests the skull belongs to anyone but Tom Thomson."

The *coup de grace* in MacGregor's investigation came courtesy of a forensic artist named Victoria Lywood. She was sent the picture of the skull and told only that the skull belonged to a male, 40 years old, who had straight black hair slightly parted to the left. As MacGregor recounts, he received Lywood's final work in an email from Williamson that bore the message, "SIT DOWN, TAKE VALIUM, OPEN SLIDE." The final image bore a strong, unshakeable resemblance to

Tom Thomson. MacGregor went on to put his findings, interwoven with his own stories of Winnie Trainor and what was known about Thomson's life into a book called *Northern Light: The Enduring Mystery of Tom Thomson*.

The totality of the evidence produced by MacGregor offered the most definitive proof to date that the skull dug up in Algonquin Park by a drunken family court judge and his buddies did, in fact, belong to Tom Thomson. The suspicions so many had about the undertaker and the work he had done in that three-hour window appeared to be validated. But what about an explanation for exactly how Thomson had died? Well, MacGregor had an answer for that too, though, unlike his theory about the remains buried in the park, there is little solid proof to back up his theory.

According to MacGregor, in 1977, he interviewed a woman by the name of Daphne Crombie. Crombie and her husband had often stayed at Canoe Lake when Thomson was there. Crombie wasn't there when Thomson died, but she returned shortly after. Crombie had been friends with Annie Fraser, who, along with her husband Shannon, ran the Mowat Lodge where Thomson often stayed. One day Annie told Daphne a story about what had happened. Annie had been cleaning up in Thomson's room when she came across a letter from Winnie Trainor. Annie decided to read the letter. It apparently indicated that Trainor was pregnant. In the letter, Trainor tells Thomson he should get himself a new suit because they needed to get married.

A confrontation ensued between Shannon Fraser and Tom Thomson when Thomson returned from the George Rowe party. The reason for the confrontation is not known, but two possibilities exist. One possibility is that Thomson demanded Shannon repay a $250 loan he had given the Frasers to buy new canoes so that he could get his new suit. Or the fight may have been a confrontation about Winnie being pregnant. Regardless, Annie Fraser told Crombie that during the ensuing tussle, Thomson fell and hit his head. Shannon Fraser, fearing Thomson had died from the injury or knowing with certainty that he had, convinced his wife to help him load Thomson's body into a canoe. The pair paddled out into the lake where they attached a weight to Thomson's body with a length of fishing line that they wrapped around his left ankle. They threw him overboard.

Crombie is quoted telling another interviewer, Ron Pittaway, in 1977:

Tom and George…they'd had a party. They were all pretty good drinkers, Tom as well. Well, they went up and had this party. They were all tight, and Tom asked Shannon Fraser for the money that he owed him because he had to go and get a new suit…Anyway, they had a fight, and Shannon hit Tom, you see, knocked him down by the grate fire, and he had a mark on his forehead…Annie [Fraser] told me all this and also Dr. MacCallum. Tom was completely knocked out by this fight. Of course, Fraser was terrified because he thought he'd killed him. This is my conception, and I don't know about other people's.

My conception is that he took Tom's body and put it into
a canoe and dropped it in the lake. That's how he died.

The biggest hole in this theory was the simple fact that Winnie Trainor was never known to have given birth to any children. In fact, she never married. But MacGregor believes he has an answer for this as well. He notes that Winnie Trainor left Canoe Lake for the winter soon after Thomson died. She was said to have been visiting friends in Philadelphia, and she returned around Easter in 1918. MacGregor speculates that she may have gone to stay at a home for unwed mothers. While this particular narrative appears to fit with what is already known about Thomson's death, there is no definitive proof that it actually happened.

Several other theories exist about what happened to Thomson, and murder is a common theme in a majority of the stories. Some still hold out that Thomson simply drowned as a result of an accident. But those who doubt this particular version of events note a few facts. First, no actual physical evidence of drowning exists because no official autopsy was performed. Second, Thomson was an experienced canoeist, so it is unlikely that he committed some sort of mistake that led to his drowning. Some have fired back with the theory that perhaps Thomson encountered a tornado or a waterspout, which is mini version of a tornado similar to a dust devil but on the water. This could have thrown him unexpectedly from his canoe and caused him to hit his head. It also could have caused the fishing line to become twisted around his leg so deliberately. Not only does this particular theory seem a bit convenient, no records exist of any tornadoes or similar weather events known to have taken place on Canoe Lake during the time frame when Thomson went missing.

The blood found in his ear has caused some to speculate Thomson could have died from some kind of head injury such as a subdural hematoma—injury to the brain. But it is unknown what could have caused the injury. Another school of thought holds out that Thomson may have simply committed suicide. With Trainor being pregnant, if he was unwilling to settle down with her, he may have simply chosen to kill himself. Detractors of this theory point to the fact that he left no suicide note; however, not everyone who takes their own life leaves a note. The fact is that there is no way to prove or disprove suicide as an explanation for Thomson's death.

No, most theories involve murder, and the cast of likely candidates and possible instruments of murder sometimes reads like a game of *Clue*. Surprisingly, very few of the older theories cast any suspicion at all on Shannon Fraser. The most likely suspect in most theories, and in the case of William Little's book, is Martin Blecher Jr., the man Thomson was seen arguing with at the George Rowe party the night before he disappeared. That theory is based almost entirely on the fact that the two argued at the party, and then Thomson left. Another theory simply states that Thomson had an enemy who was known as an American draft dodger, and that the two fought the night before Tom died. As to how he was killed, the possible murder weapons could be a gun or a canoe paddle. A gun is often cited as the most likely, given the presence of the small hole in the skull that is believed to belong to Thomson.

Apparently, at least one person near the lake claimed to have heard a gunshot sometime that night, but no other evidence substantiates the claim. Some even point to the fact that Winnie Trainor was not allowed to view the body of Tom Thomson before it was buried in the first grave at Canoe Lake as proof of those involved trying to cover up a murder. There is also the issue that neither Dr. Howland, who inspected the body, nor ranger Robinson, who was also present, made any mention of the presence of a bullet hole. They both indicated the presence of a bruise on Thomson's left temple, but that's all. Some say the body may have been so bloated and distorted from decay and its time in the lake that the bullet hole could have been covered up by swollen skin and flesh. Given the brevity of Dr. Howland's examination, this is a possibility, but it seems strange that a bullet hole in the head would have been overlooked.

The paddle is cited as a weapon of opportunity given that Thomson and many others on the lake were avid canoeists. Additional proof is often cited in the form of an interview from another person who was once on the lake at the same time as Blecher. That person claimed Blecher took a swing at him with one of his paddles.

Others have speculated that Thomson was shot and killed by poachers after Thomson stumbled across their illegal activities. Unfortunately, no real evidence supports this theory.

The Tom Thomson Memorial Cairn, Canoe Lake, Algonquin Park

Another, even more outlandish, theory states that foreign agents operating in Canada during World War I killed Thomson. Specifically, they believe that a group of German saboteurs was planning to blow up some train tracks in the area when Thomson accidentally stumbled upon them in the woods. So the agents were forced to kill him to silence him.

Martin Blecher, Jr. features in the espionage theory as well, as ranger Mark Robinson actually wrote in his journal two months prior to Thomson's death:

Martin Blecher, Jr., left this morning for St. Louis. I am of the opinion he is a German spy.

However, those historians who have examined this
theory critically have come to the conclusion that while Blecher
might not have been a nice guy, no evidence supports the claim
that he was a spy. Any conclusion that he was a German spy was
more likely a result of the "spymania" culture that dominated
the Allied countries during the war, along with the anti-German
prejudice prevalent at the time. Historian Peter Webb of the
University of Ottawa wrote an essay entitled *Martin Blecher:
Tom Thomson's Murderer or Victim of Wartime Prejudice?* In the
essay, Webb writes:

> *Blecher was a recluse, an alcoholic and may have been
> quarrelsome on occasion, but he was also helpful and hos-
> pitable in times of crisis....Many of his neighbours in the
> remote village of Mowat, Ontario, feared him, but it is
> probable that the fear was exacerbated by his German
> background at a time when the spectre of German sabo-
> tage and espionage loomed large in wartime Canada.*

We have a better idea of where Tom Thomson is buried.
It appears he is, in fact, buried in Algonquin Park, even though
that grave is apparently unmarked. Exactly how Thomson died,
however, is still a mystery, and his death may never be solved.

The Ghost Ship of Northumberland Strait

~

For the last 220 years, sightings of a ghost ship have been reported in the Northumberland Strait. The sightings are typically consistent, describing a schooner with either three or four masts flying white sails. The intriguing part is that these sails apparently catch fire as onlookers watch.

Local legend holds that a sighting of the ghost ship is the equivalent of a storm warning. But the ship has apparently taken in a few people. More than a few mariners, seeing the sails on fire, have chased the ship in an attempt to save the crew. In one instance in 1900, a crew took off after the ship in a rowboat for a rescue, but the ship later completely vanished, and no wreck was ever found.

There have been a few attempts to explain the sighting scientifically. Francis Ganong, a New Brunswick scientist, suggested in 1905 that the ghost ship sighting was actually some kind of natural electrical occurrence. Another attempt to explain the ghost ship points to the possibility of moonlight reflecting off the fog.

The most recent sighting of the ghost ship is said to have taken place in 2008. In June 2014, Canada Post decided to commemorate the ghost ship with its own stamp, which was issued as part of a series of stamps featuring Canadian ghost stories.

~

Chapter 3

The Black Donnellys

~

Few crimes in the history of Canada match the brutality and viciousness of the murders of almost an entire family. What makes the crime even more unique and sensational is the fact that, not only has it been proven that the family in question was the victim of a lynch mob, but that despite witness evidence, no one was ever convicted of the crime.

The victims were the members of a family of Irish immigrants who had come to Canada in the hopes of finding a new life. But in the years after they arrived in the region that would eventually become Ontario, the family succeeded in turning an entire town against them. Whether it involved murder, questionable business practices, alleged sabotage or outright theft, in the end, the victims found themselves squared off against an entire population who felt they had to take matters into their own hands.

That family was the Donnellys. Because of their Irish heritage and the unique mix of other Irish immigrants that called the Biddulph area home, the family would be later described as the Black Donnellys. The murders were all the more brutal because the mob made no distinction between man and woman when it decided to mete out its own arbitrary and brutal brand of justice. In its eyes, anyone associated with the Donnellys deserved to die. This is the story of how one family managed to turn an entire community against it, and how a mob was able to get away with murder.

~

Canada wasn't yet an independent country in the 1840s, but to many it was seen as a land of hope and promise. The vast country was especially attractive to those in Ireland who were Catholic because all of the land in Ireland was owned by British and Irish Protestants. So many of those who couldn't own land in Ireland looked to pre-Confederation Canada as a place where they might be able to live a better life.

James Donnelly was one of those people. Sometime in the mid 1840s—some accounts say 1842 while others 1844, or between 1845-46—Donnelly immigrated to Upper Canada from Tipperary, Ireland. He brought with him his wife Johannah, as well as their first-born son James Jr. Shortly after they arrived in Canada, Johannah gave birth to another son, William. This son, however, was born with a deformed foot, an affliction that would later earn him the moniker "Clubfoot Will."

The family first lived in London, but James wanted to find a healthy swath of land for his family. So sometime around 1845 or 1846, James and the family moved from London to Biddulph, a community northwest of London. If there was something pre-Confederation Canada had plenty of, it was land. But James had a problem. He didn't have much money, and he couldn't afford any of the land in the area. So he resorted to a tactic fairly common in frontier days; he became a squatter. He found some land that he liked, about 100 acres, and simply moved on to it. The land, located on lot 18, concession 6, was owned by John Grace, an absentee landlord.

James set to work building a crude home for his family. He also worked the land tirelessly to clear it for his own purposes. In the years they lived on the land, the family grew. John Donnelly was born in 1847, followed by Patrick in 1849, Michael in 1850, Robert in 1853 and Thomas in 1854. The Donnellys also had one daughter, Jenny, who was born in 1857.

But before Jenny was born, John Grace decided, in 1855, to sell his land. There were two men involved in the transaction—Michael Maher and Patrick Farrell. The problem, of course, was the Donnellys were still living on the land, had cleared a large part of it over the 10 years they had been living on it and weren't about to leave. This led to problems between James Donnelly Sr. and Patrick Farrell, which culminated in one point in Donnelly being charged with firing a shot at Farrell. The matter went to court, with Farrell and Maher seeking to have the Donnellys ejected from the property. In the end, Farrell decided to let Donnelly keep 50 acres, which was considerably less than what the Donnellys had cleared for themselves.

Yet despite his decision to sell the land to James Donnelly, Farrell was bitter about what had taken place. The growing tension between the two men came to a head later in 1857, during a logging bee. Several men from the area had assembled to help William Maloney do some work on land in the area. Historical accounts of the incident state that many of the men present had been drinking heavily, including Farrell and Donnelly. A verbal confrontation occurred between the two men that quickly escalated into a fight. In the end, James Sr. picked up a handspike and threw it at Farrell. The spike hit Farrell squarely in the head. Farrell died two days later from the wound sustained from the handspike, and Donnelly became a man wanted for murder.

Rather than give himself up, James Donnelly Sr. disappeared before the local constables could arrest him. When officers went to the Donnelly house looking for him, Johannah refused to speak to them. No one else seemed to know where James Sr. was. He successfully evaded the police for more than two years by hiding in plain site. He alternated between living in the family barn or in the wild nearby with sleeping in the homes of friends and acquaintances when the weather grew cold. He still worked the fields, but disguised himself by dressing in his wife's clothes. He continued doing so for two years before he grew tired of living in hiding and decided to turn himself in.

His trial was held in nearby Goderich, where he was found guilty of murder and sentenced to death. His execution was to take place on September 17, 1858. But Johannah refused to believe her husband would actually be executed, so she started a petition asking for clemency. Johanna spent the entire summer looking for people to sign it. Her efforts were successful. In July her petition was accepted, and James' execution was commuted to a seven-year prison sentence at the Kingston Penitentiary. Johannah took out a mortgage on the farm in order to survive, and she was able to keep the farm going until James Sr. was released from prison in 1865.

The Donnelly boys played an instrumental role in helping Johannah keep the farm and work the fields, but they also began to cause problems locally. The boys were accused of and charged with scores of crimes, but few of the charges ever resulted in convictions. In 1869 William was charged with larceny but was later acquitted. That same year William and James Jr. were charged with robbing a nearby post office, but they were also both acquitted.

Eventually, the boys began to make their own lives as well. In 1870, James Jr. moved to Michigan while Patrick trained in wagon and carriage making and actually got married. John managed a nearby saloon while Robert, Michael and Thomas started farming another property in Biddulph. William mostly helped his parents with their farm.

In 1871 the boys decided to venture into the business world, working for a local stage line. Stages, at the time, were the fastest way to travel between communities, and the work could be quite lucrative. In fact, the boys became so interested in working stages that, when the stage line they had been working for folded, William decided to start his own line, hiring brothers Robert and Thomas to drive. They even joined up with another local stage line in an effort to boost business.

But the stage line business was incredibly competitive, and the Donnelly boys soon found themselves embroiled in accusations of sabotage. The reports of sabotage began to mount, both against the Donnellys and their competitors. In 1875, one of the stages belonging to competitor Patrick Flanagan was destroyed when a wheel of the coach fell off. The resulting accident killed the stage driver, William Brooks, and sabotage was widely suspected. In a second accident, a Flanagan-operated stage cut off one of the Donnelly's stages, causing passengers to fall out of the coach. The courts ordered Flanagan to pay damages to the Donnellys and the Donnellys to pay damages to two of their passengers who had been injured when thrown from the coach.

The mayhem didn't end there. Later that same year, someone set Flanagan's stables on fire, killing his horses. One of his stages was also burned. Later that same year, Flanagan was assaulted. The Donnellys were accused of setting the stables on fire, but they were later acquitted and one of their accusers was later charged with perjury.

Those weren't the only legal troubles the Donnelly boys faced. James Jr. and Thomas were accused of robbing another man, but they were never charged. William Donnelly was later charged with perjury in an incident in which he helped his brother Robert avoid being arrested for threatening another man. In 1976, a riot broke out when three constables showed up at a wedding the Donnellys were attending to arrest several of the boys. All of the boys save for Michael escaped originally. Michael was actually captured and lodged at the Lucan Hotel, but he also managed to escape. In a separate incident, William and John were convicted of assaulting a constable and sentenced to prison, but William was discharged due to illness.

The problems didn't end there. Starting in 1877, it seemed that the Donnellys were being blamed for every problem that cropped up in Biddulph. Violence was on the rise, and everyone in the area was certain the Donnellys were responsible. Even the untimely death of James Donnelly Jr. from illness didn't arouse much sympathy for the family.

As it happened, the boys were now out of work because the creation of the new rail line in the area, which could take more passengers between communities faster, led to the bankruptcy of their stage line. The family was also feuding with new individuals in town. A man by the name of James Carroll was causing problems for the family, going so far as charging the boys with assault and their mother, Johannah, with using "abusive language." And Robert Donnelly was sentenced to prison after he was convicted of taking a shot at a local constable. He was forced to serve two years at Kingston Penitentiary.

Even the local priest was causing problems for the Donnellys. In an effort to try to bring some more order to the community, the new priest created a Peace Society or Association. He asked all the members of the community to pledge their support to the new association. Those who pledged their support were required to allow their homes to be searched for stolen property. It was noted by almost everyone that the Donnellys did not pledge their support to the cause.

Postcard of three members of the Vigilance Society: left to right, John Kennedy, James Carroll, Martin McLaughlin

A splinter group formed within the new peace association, this group more focused on the Donnellys than on general peace and order. It was called the Vigilance Society. Many of the Donnellys' neighbours joined the group, and a key member was James Carroll, the Donnellys newest nemesis. Carroll even went so far as to become a constable for the area, and in so doing, he promised to rid the community of the family.

Carroll immediately went after the family by trying to arrest Thomas on an old charge, but the family was able to warn Thomas and help him escape. One of the brothers, John, was charged with helping Thomas escape and with perjury, but he was subsequently acquitted. The incident just added to the Vigilance Society's hatred of the family, and the group began openly encouraging locals to loathe the Donnellys. Even news of the violent death of one of the boys did nothing to generate sympathy for the family. Michael Donnelly moved to St. Thomas for work, but he was killed in a fight with another man in nearby Waterford. The family was even accused of burning down a local barn even though most of the boys were at a wedding when it took place. The Vigilance Society subsequently charged James Sr. and Johannah with the crime.

On the night of February 3, 1880, James and Johannah Donnelly were at their home, preparing for their trial on the charge of barn burning. The trial was supposed to take place the next day in Granton. At the same time as the Donnellys were winding down at home, the Vigilance Society was meeting at the nearby Cedar Swamp Schoolhouse. The members of the Vigilance Society were drunk and angry. Their hatred of the Donnellys had reached a boiling point and, fuelled by large quantities of liquor, the group decided that it was time to take matters into their own hands. The group asked one of its members, James Feeheley, to go over to the Donnelly's home under the guise of dropping by for a visit to spy on who was at the home at that time.

James and Johannah were not at home alone. Thomas was there, as was their niece Bridget who was visiting from Ireland. The couple had also hired Johnny O'Connor, a local teenager, to help out on the farm and mind their pigs while they were out in Granton the next day for their trial. John Donnelly had been at the home, but then he headed over to William's house to borrow a sleigh for the next day to take the family to court. Rather than head back, John decided instead to spend the night at William's.

Back at the Donnelly house, everyone was getting ready for bed. James Sr., ever a traditionalist, informed everyone he was going to bed and informed Johnny O'Connor that the two of them would be sleeping in the same room. Johannah would be sleeping with Bridget in a room next to James' room, while Thomas took to a room near the back of the house. Shortly after James headed to bed, James Feeheley showed up, spoke with Bridget and Johannah then left. He reported back to the Vigilance Society, who set out shortly after midnight.

The Vigilance Society's members headed for the Donnelly house. Their original plan had been straightforward, though monstrously illegal. The plan was to raid the house, handcuff all the Donnelly men and take them away. They would then hang them all from the neck until they confessed to their crimes. It's unclear if they were planning to kill them as a result of hanging them by the neck or if this was just intended as a scare tactic in order to get them to confess to their criminal activities. But once they reached the Donnelly home, something changed. James Carroll took the lead. As the rest of the Vigilance Society surrounded the house, Carroll went inside and placed a pair of handcuffs on a sleeping Thomas Donnelly, who awoke only when Carroll announced that he was under arrest. Carroll then checked the home for John Donnelly, who was nowhere to be found. He next went into the front bedroom, where he roused James Sr. The commotion woke Johannah and Bridget, who came downstairs and started to stir the fire to warm the room.

James Sr. was overheard to ask Carroll, "What have you got against us now?"

Carroll replied only that they were being charged with a crime. Thomas grew increasingly angry and asked Carroll to read the warrant aloud. At that moment, Carroll gave some sort of signal to the Vigilance Society to storm the house. However, the plan to take all the men away and try to elicit confessions from them quickly evaporated in a wave of drunken rage. Once the group entered the house, they started beating on everyone they could see. James was quickly felled, as was Johannah. Thomas managed to slip free and make a run for the door, but

Postcard with a sketch of the Donnelly homestead made up after the massacre of the family members: (left) James Donnelly and (possibly) John Donnelly; (right) Johanna Donnelly and Robert Donnelly

someone was lying in wait on the other side of the door and ran him through with a pitchfork. He was carried back inside and placed on the floor.

The group continued searching the house and found Bridget hiding upstairs. She was beaten and carried back downstairs. They searched the home one more time in the hopes of finding John Donnelly, but found no sign of him. The group set fire to James and Johannah's bed before leaving. The fire quickly engulfed the building and the bodies inside.

The Vigilance Society wasn't done. They were still looking for John, and they thought they knew where to find him. They struck off for William's residence, arriving some time around 2:00 AM, again surrounding the area so no one could get away. Perhaps suffering from the first twinges of regret over what they had done at the Donnelly home, the group decided instead to try and get those inside to come out to meet them. They started by descending on the barn where they killed William Donnelly's stallion. But the barn was too far away, and William didn't hear the frenzied cries of the dying animal. So the group stood outside and started to call for William, also apparently yelling "Fire!" in the hopes of flushing him from the house.

Eventually, someone did emerge from the house. But it wasn't William. John Donnelly woke up before his brother and decided to investigate the source of the racket. But the Vigilance Society didn't give John the chance to identify himself. No sooner did John step outside than several gunshots boomed through the night. John fell, hit several times in the chest and groin.

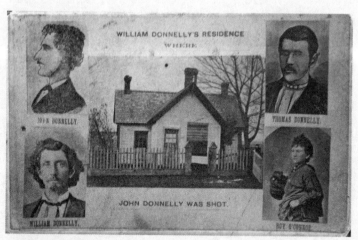

Postcard photo of William Donnelly's home; photos or sketches: (left) John Donnelly and William Donnelly; (right) Thomas Donnelly and Boy (Johnny) O'Connor

The sound of gunshots roused everyone inside. William hid below the window as members of the Vigilance Society approached the house and tried peering through the dark windows to see if anyone else was inside. John's body was surreptitiously pulled inside, but he died shortly after. For William and the others hiding inside the house all was quiet for three hours until one voice, said to belong to James Feeheley, was heard to say to the mob, "There's been enough bloodshed tonight, boys. Let's go home." The mob subsequently turned and left.

William became an important witness to the death of his brother. But unbeknownst at first to the Vigilance Society, another witness survived the attack at the James Donnelly home and had seen a great deal of what had happened. Johnny

O'Connor had been sleeping in the bedroom with James Sr. when the mob had descended on the home. Apparently, no one had noticed him, even though he had at one point handed James Sr. his jacket right in front of Carroll, shortly before the beatings started. When he heard the commotion begin, O'Connor hid under the bed. And when the mob moved on through the rest of the house, Johnny made a run for the stairs, following Bridget as she tried to hide. But when Bridget reached the top of the stairs, she slammed the door shut behind her, trapping Johnny on the stairs. He tried the door, but when it wouldn't open, he dashed back down the stairs and hid under a bed. He managed to keep himself hidden as Bridget was carried down and murdered, then still managed to stay calm enough to remain under the bed even as the mob set the house on fire. Once he was certain all the attackers had gone, Johnny ran for his life.

The police eventually heard about what had taken place, and they descended on the Donnelly homestead and put all the remains they could find into one casket. By February 5, James Carroll and 12 others were arrested and charged with the murder of James Sr., Johannah, Bridget and John Donnelly. Johnny O'Connor and William Donnelly would become the most important witnesses for the prosecution.

The trial was scheduled for October 1880. Several of the people involved tried to stop Johnny O'Connor from testifying, even going so far as burning his father's house to the ground before the first trial. But, based largely on Johnny's testimony, six of those charged were committed to trial after a preliminary inquiry. The prosecution tried to have the location of the first

Johnny O'Connor, who testified as an eyewitness
to the massacre

trial moved; they felt that there was so much ill will built up towards the Donnellys locally that finding an impartial jury would be impossible. But the judge refused, and the first trial took place in London from October 4 to October 9, 1880.

O'Connor told the court how James Sr. had asked him to spend the night, and to sleep in the same room as him. The last thing he heard before he fell asleep was a familiar voice:

I went to sleep after I heard (James) Feeheley talking. I slept next to the wall; the head of the bed was towards the front of the house, and there was no curtains around it.

Next thing he knew, he awoke when James Sr. got out of bed. O'Connor saw Carroll in the living room. James Sr. was getting dressed. He asked Johnny to pass him his jacket, which Johnny may have been using as a pillow. He noticed that Johannah was up and stoking the fire, and that she was calling for Bridget. He noted that Thomas was in the living room as well. Johnny heard Thomas turned to speak to Carroll:

> *Tom told him to read the warrant. Carroll said there was lots of time for that. Then in a few minutes a whole crowd jumped in and commenced hammering them with sticks and spade; then Tom ran out into the front room and outside. I saw him run out and Bridget ran upstairs and I ran after her and she shut the door and I ran back again in the room and got under the bed behind the clothesbasket. Then they started hammering Tom outside.*

Johnny could barely fit under the bed. He figured the bed was little more than half a metre off the floor, and he noted there were no curtains covering the space under the bed. But he could still see and hear a great deal of what was going on. The crowd carried Thomas, who had, by then, been run through with the pitchfork, back into the house and threw him on the floor.

Johnny testified:

> *Then someone said, "Hit that fellow with a spade and break his skull open." Then the fellow hit him three or four whacks with the spade. When Tom was outside I heard him say, "Oh! Oh! Oh!" I did not see them hit Tom with the spade, but heard them; then some of them told the fellow*

that had the light to bring it here to where Tom was. He brought the light, and they were doing something to Tom.

The light clearly illuminated two faces—Thomas Ryder, whose barn the Donnellys had been accused of burning down, and John Purtell. But even though they had James Sr., Johannah and Thomas, the mob went looking for someone else. They found Bridget, the niece visiting from Ireland.

Then some of them asked where was the girl; another one answered, "Look upstairs"; then they went upstairs, and I saw some of them too, but did not know any of them; then they came down.

The next thing Johnny knew, the mob was setting the house on fire. They poured coal oil all over the bed under which he was hiding, ignited it and left.

Johnny continued:

Then I got out from under the bed and put on my pants and tried to quench the fire with my coat; I hit the fire with my coat: I then heard Tom breathing, then I went out to the front room and saw Tom dead on the floor; then I ran out to the kitchen and tramped on the old woman [Mrs. Donnelly]; there was a light from the fire in my bed, also from Tom's bed: the door of Tom's room was open, and the door from the front room into the kitchen: the old woman was lying between the door from the front room into the kitchen and the kitchen door going outside.

Johnny ran to Pat Whalen's house nearby.

He explained to the court what Carroll, Ryder and Purtell had been wearing that night:

Purtell had dark clothes, Ryder a peaked cap and Carroll had grey pants; their faces were not blackened. I saw one man with his face blackened and a long coat on, a middling sized man. Carroll saw me in bed; he looked right at me, and I saw him looking right at me for a while; he did not speak to me. I did not see anyone strike the Donnellys; I only heard them.

William Donnelly was also called to give testimony to the court about what had happened at his house. William explained that he had not heard any of the commotion; his brother John heard it. William woke up when John came out of his room.

William testified:

He couldn't go to the kitchen without going through my room; I didn't speak to John. He said I wonder whose hollering fire and rapping the door; he kept right on and opened the door. When John opened the door going into the kitchen from my room, I heard them holler, 'Fire! Fire! Open the door Will!'

John had only just stepped outside when William heard gunshots.

I then heard two shots in rapid succession almost together; John fell back against the door from my bedroom to the kitchen; the distance between the kitchen door and my

*bedroom is about six or seven feet; his head came down to
the jam of the door.*

William lay next to the door, but he could see out
a nearby window. He named three men who he clearly saw
through that window: John Kennedy, James Carroll and James
Ryder. He added that he saw three more people standing nearby,
two of whom he identified as Patrick Ryder and Michael
Heenan:

> *I couldn't swear positively to them. I don't speak positively
> as to them. I speak positively as to John Kennedy, James
> Carroll and James Ryder; these persons are well known
> to me.*

Despite having solid eye witness testimony provided by
both Johnny O'Connor and William Donnelly, the jury did not
move to convict any of the accused of the murders. Four jurors
thought the men were guilty, seven wanted to acquit the men
and one was undecided. The members of the Vigilance Society
all had friends and family who provided them with solid alibis
for the night of the murders. The prosecution's concerns about
being unable to find an impartial jury were also borne out
when several jurors later said that they were afraid of what
would happen to them if they had voted to convict the men.
One juror went so far as to declare that he wouldn't have found
James Carroll guilty, even if he had personally witnessed all of
the killings.

The prosecution successfully got a second trial, and it happened quickly. The second trial ran from January 24 to February 2, 1881. Johnny O'Connor was again called to testify, and he is described in newspaper accounts of the day as performing well. The problem for O'Connor was his mother. She was also called to the stand to testify, but the defence did a good job of using her to poke holes in Johnny's credibility. When she was called to the stand, she was unable to say how old her son was. The defence also called into question a recent trip she had made to Toronto to visit with the deputy attorney general.

The O'Connor family was in trouble financially, given that their house had been deliberately burned down several months before in an effort to prevent Johnny from testifying. The defence implied that she had been meeting with the deputy attorney general in an effort to get them to pay her son for providing his testimony in the trial. Yet O'Connor's mother did not give any explanation for the meeting. She also got into a disagreement with someone immediately prior to her testimony so that when she took the stand, she was agitated, greatly impacting her testimony. As a result, the jury again failed to convict anyone of the murders.

None of those involved ever again faced trial. The surviving Donnellys actually later became friends with Feeheleys, the family of James who had spied on the Donnellys the night of the slayings. And despite the fact that the Feeheleys fled to Michigan after the attack, they were extradited back to Canada but never faced trial.

Bob Donnelly and his nephew James Michael (son of Michael) in front of the house built after the massacre. The house is still there today but with additions on the front, back and side.

~

The surviving Donnellys tried to carry on with their lives. William moved to Ohio in 1882 to work in the coalmines, while Patrick stayed in the wagon-making business. Robert ran a hauling business out of Glencoe while Jennie was married off to a local constable. William returned to Canada in 1883 and became a constable for a few years but eventually resigned and opened a hotel in Appin.

Problems still cropped up with the Donnellys from time to time. Robert became known for his opposition to the preaching and tactics of the Salvation Army, and in 1885 he was suspected when the local barracks of the Salvation Army were set on fire. In 1897, William died of natural causes. In 1908,

Robert was committed to a psychiatric hospital before dying of natural causes in 1911. Patrick died in 1914, with Jennie following two years later.

The Donnelly killings endured in Canadian history as one of the country's most horrific crimes. The family eventually became known as the Black Donnellys. The reason for the moniker has to do with the family's Irish roots and the roots of other Irish families in the area, which might have also factored into the slayings because of the considerable amount of religious tension in the area. Irish Protestants were the majority in the region, and the Catholics resented it.

Some of the Catholics who were opposed to Irish Protestants identified themselves as Whiteboys, a secret society of Catholics. The Donnellys were actually known as Blackfeet, a group of citizens who were friendly with the Protestants. The Donnellys had actually attracted the ire of local Catholics when James Sr. made a financial contribution towards the construction of an Anglican church in the area. Some have subsequently argued that the slayings of the Donnellys were actually a direct result of the religious tension in the area, regardless of how the Donnellys were perceived in the community.

Chapter 4
The Granger Affair

~

There was a time where it seemed like most people who talked about UFOs and encounters with aliens and even being abducted by extraterrestrial beings all seemed to come from the same part of the world. Maybe they had southern accents, but they all thought that the best place to share their stories was on a daytime talk show that was more interested in shock value than on actually sharing real stories. But a look at the record from even across Canada shows that UFO sightings are, while not common, not rare either. As a reporter with the *St. Albert Gazette*, I once wrote a feature story that detailed some of the UFO stories from the Internet that originated just in St. Albert and the surrounding region. So if a small suburb of Edmonton can generate stories about close encounters with the unexplained, then imagine what else can be found out there just in our own backyard. I interviewed one man who was the host of an Internet radio show and website devoted to UFOs. Statistics reported in the mainstream press appear to be proof that we are seeing something out there, and we are seeing it more and more often. In 2012, Canadians reported 1981 sightings, almost double the previous record of

1004 sightings from four years earlier. Some 7.5 per cent of the 2012 total were reported as "unexplained." A search for Canada and UFO sightings turns up websites that list dozens of reported sightings each year right up to the present day.

Some Canadians have also reported being kidnapped by aliens. They are somehow transported aboard a strange ship, sometimes experimented on or sometimes simply observed before being returned to Earth. Others have so-called "missing time" experiences, where one minute they are engaged in an activity, and suddenly it is several hours later and they have no recollection of anything that happened during the intervening hours.

It's not often; however, that someone leaves a note for their family, indicating they are leaving on a journey through the solar system, and then they actually disappear and never return. But such is the case of one Canadian, Granger Taylor, whose disappearance to this day does not appear to be adequately explained. Depending on who you believe, it may be that Taylor took his own life, succumbed to the elements or is actually exploring the stars on board an interstellar spaceship.

From all accounts, Granger Taylor was always a little different. He was born on October 7, 1948, in Duncan, BC, which is located on the southeast side of Vancouver Island, south of Somenos Lake. His mother, Grace, and stepfather, Jim, raised Granger. His stepfather apparently treated Granger as if he were his own son. Two things about Granger were immediately apparent—he was different, and he was something of a genius. From a young age he demonstrated an incredible aptitude for mechanics. He taught himself to repair and even build various items. He stunned everyone when, at age 14, he built a single-cylinder vehicle that was later exhibited at the Duncan Forest Museum. When he was 17, he overhauled and repaired to working condition a bulldozer that no one else had been able to restore.

In 1969, the story goes that he found an abandoned steam locomotive that had been abandoned in the bush since the 1930s. Many of its parts had been scavenged over the years, especially during World War II, and trees and brush were growing through it. But Granger worked his way through the bush, hauled that locomotive out of there and over the course of a few years actually restored it to working condition. In 1973, the BC government purchased the engine and sent it out on a tour with its Museum Train before putting it on display at the BC Forest Discovery Centre. And if that wasn't enough, Granger went even further, building a replica of a Curtiss P-40 Kittyhawk fighter plane, the type used during World War II. The plane was later put on display on the side of the road outside an antique store on the Island Highway.

Yet despite his incredible aptitude for all things mechanical, Granger apparently decided that school just wasn't where he belonged. He dropped out in Grade 8 and got his first job soon after as a mechanic's helper for one of his neighbours. After a year in the job, he struck out on his own, working as a welder, a mechanic or repairing heavy-duty machinery. He grew to a towering two metres (6 feet, 3 inches) and weighed an imposing 113 kilograms (250 pounds). Many said he had the build of a professional wrestler, which proved to be apt because Granger loved wrestling and had even built his own ring on his parents' property. However, he earned the moniker "Gentle Ben" for the shy, polite way he carried himself. His parents yard became known locally as the Sleepy Hollow Museum as he continued to accumulate old tractors, bulldozers, cars and all manner of wrecks that he could find in the area around Duncan. He eventually studied for and earned his pilot's licence and, with a partner, purchased his very own airplane.

Yet Granger suddenly became obsessed with UFOs and aliens, and in the 1970s he started collecting and reading all the books he could find on the topic. He then spent six months of his life building a flying saucer. He took two large satellite dishes and welded them together into the shape of a spaceship that was 4.6 metres in diameter. The UFO wasn't just for show; the inside became a retreat of sorts for Granger. Some nights he would sleep inside. He even moved in an old sofa, a wood-burning stove and a plywood sleeping ledge, and he spent time inside reading his books.

By all accounts his obsession with UFOs soon shifted slightly; he was now more interested in exactly how UFOs were powered and propelled through space. It was a difficult project to tackle. At the time, all anyone really knew about UFOs were what they read in books. So all Granger had to work from were the second- and third-hand accounts of others and what they saw. Perhaps it was inevitable, given his talents with mechanical objects, that Granger found himself tackling this new challenge. By all reports, it consumed him. Whenever he socialized with his friends, Granger inevitably steered the conversation back to the subjects of UFOs, aliens and propulsion.

And then, one night in the fall of 1980, Granger was lying in bed when, according to a friend, he was contacted.

"He said it happened when he was in bed. He lay there and got mental communications with somebody from another galaxy," said Bob Nielsen, a long-time friend. "He couldn't see them. I said they can't just be mental, but he said it was like they were talking just to him and to his mind. He was asking questions about the means for powering their crafts. The only thing they'd tell him was it was magnetic."

Granger was convinced that his experience was authentic. A few days after the first contact, Granger began telling everyone that the beings that had contacted him had invited him along on a space journey. When pressed for details, Granger said he was awaiting instructions and had been told that he would find out at the end of the month exactly when he would be picked up and where he needed to be to catch "his ride."

His friends, although skeptical, apparently didn't try to do anything to dissuade Granger about what he believed was going to happen. They even went so far as to accompany him on a trip for a going-away party of sorts. His friends humoured him, no doubt assuming that this was just Granger being Granger and that nothing would actually happen. Yet as the date grew near, Granger kept the actual details of his trip a secret, refusing to divulge it to anyone, not even to his parents, with whom he was still living.

On November 28, 1980, Granger walked into his stepfather's bedroom and sat down to talk. His mother was away on vacation in Hawaii, and Granger had something he wanted to say. He told his stepfather how grateful and appreciative he was for all Jim had done for him over the years. If Jim was suspicious about Granger intentions or why he was bothering to share his feelings at that specific time, he didn't say anything.

The following day, a nasty storm was forecast to lay siege to Vancouver Island later in the evening. It turned out that November 29 was the day that Granger would finally strike off on his voyage, yet there was little appreciable difference in how he spent his day. The last person to see him was a woman named Linda Baron, who was working in the kitchen of Bob's Diner, where he stopped for supper. Granger often ate at Bob's Diner. According to Baron, Granger came in and sat by himself. Despite the repeated warnings of the impending storm, Granger was not wearing a winter coat or jacket of any kind. He was wearing a brown-knitted sweater, zipped at the front, over his omnipresent black t-shirt, with jeans and logger boots. The coat he usually wore was found a few days later inside the doghouse he had built for his enormous Newfoundland dog, Lady. Granger left the restaurant at approximately 6:30 PM. No one ever saw him again.

When Jim returned home from work later that day, he found a note tacked to his bedroom door. The words were clearly written in Granger's writing. The exact text of the note read:

> Dear Mother and Father,
>
> I have gone away to walk aboard an alien spaceship, as re-occurring dreams assured a 42-month interstellar voyage to explore the vast universe, then return.
>
> I am leaving behind all my possessions to you as I will no longer require the use of any. Please use the instructions in my will as a guide to help.
>
> Love,
>
> Granger

The paper on which the note was written contained, on its reverse side, a contour map of Waterloo Mountain, located 30 kilometres west of the Taylors' property. It is not known if the map and choice of paper for his farewell note was meant to have any connection to Granger's disappearance.

Granger also left a will behind, two actually. Curiously, in the document, the word "deceased" was scratched out and replaced with the word "departed."

That night, as forecast, a massive storm walloped Duncan. The winds were described in sources dating to that night using words such as "gale force" and "hurricane," even though hurricanes technically can't happen in the Pacific Ocean (they are called typhoons). The storm was so powerful it knocked out power across Duncan and other parts of the island, plunging everyone into darkness.

Jim didn't bother to wait around and immediately contacted the RCMP, who began the search for Granger right away. Yet despite following as many different avenues of investigation as possible, they were unable to turn up anything of any significance related to Granger's disappearance. His parents went so far as to leave their backdoor open every night in the event that Granger would return. He never did. They even ensured the door was open on May 29, 1984, the date that the "42-month interstellar voyage" was calculated to come to an end. Still Granger never returned. The only other thing of note missing was the pale blue Datsun truck he had driven away in that day. His bank account still had $10,000 in it when he left, and it was never touched. The RCMP focused on finding the vehicle when all other leads ran out, expecting it would turn up somewhere.

"One would expect the car at least to be found," RCMP Corporal Mike Demchuk was reported as saying in one news story about Granger's disappearance. "You just don't get rid of something that large without someone knowing about it."

The Taylors even took out newspaper ads intermittently, offering $100 for anyone who found the truck, but to no avail. The licence plate expired in 1981, but no one tried to renew it.

The RCMP, meanwhile, were left with pursuing more unconventional leads in an effort to find Granger. They checked with the passport office to see if any activity had been recorded on his passport but had no luck. They checked with what was then called Revenue Canada and Unemployment Insurance to see if Granger had in any way taken part in a transaction that might have registered with either department but came up blank. They entered Granger's name into a national computer database in the hopes that he might turn up somewhere in Canada someday, but no one ever called back. They even went so far as alerting the motor vehicle branch in Victoria to Granger's driver's licence, which expired in October 1985. No one ever showed up to try to renew it.

For all intents and purposes, Granger Taylor had disappeared. And when stories began to emerge about the note he had left behind, coupled with the fact that no trace of Granger was ever found anywhere, people began to speculate about just what might have happened to him. Some individuals, including at least one university professor, were convinced that Granger had, in fact, been taken aboard a spaceship on a journey to the stars. While many ufologists noted that Vancouver Island and the community of Duncan were well off the usual routes UFOs appeared to take, sightings were not unheard of. In the southern part of the island, at least 20 sightings of UFOs or other unexplained objects were reported between 1980 and 1985. Many of those sightings came from the Mount Prevost area, not far from Duncan.

Granger's disappearance was even linked with one particular story of a UFO sighting, 10 years earlier. On December 31, 1969, at 11:59 PM, at Cowichan District Hospital in Duncan, BC, a nurse named Doreen Kendall was helping some patients when she looked out the window and saw a "Saturn-shaped" object hovering outside the window of the room where she was working. She could see inside the object two occupants that had humanoid characteristics. Those who point to this particular story say that the aliens in that craft might have been intrigued by Granger, who had gone so far as to build his own UFO and who was so mechanically skilled and adept, that they might very well have contacted him.

The truth, unfortunately, might have absolutely nothing to do with aliens and UFOs, and might be much more tragic. A clipping retrieved from the Internet published in the *Montreal Gazette*, dated March 31, 1986, seems to detail the most likely fate to befall Granger Taylor. Entitled "Bones may be those of UFO fan who 'blasted off'," the brief states that pieces of a truck were recovered from "the site of a dynamite blast" on Mount Prevost, six kilometres northwest of Duncan. The article states that, along with the pieces of a truck, two pieces of bone were found inside the crater, which had been discovered by forestry crews working in the area. A pathologist confirmed the bones were human. While nothing is stated definitively in the news brief, other Internet sources refer to the vehicle's VIN being recovered, and that the number matched Granger's vehicle. But some of those sources report that the truck was pink in colour, when it was known the truck Granger was driving the day he disappeared was light blue.

The *Gazette* brief also states that "[Granger] had taken dynamite, used for blasting tree stumps, from his parents'

Duncan-area farm." Some have said Granger committed suicide. But those who believe something else happened to Granger point to the note as proof against the suicide theory, wondering why someone intent on killing themselves would go so far as to write a note saying they were leaving on a 42-month interstellar voyage. It would be, they say, a cruel hoax.

Still others discount both the idea of him being transported aboard a spaceship by aliens and that the truck remains found belonged to his vehicle. Instead they speculate that Granger may have simply wandered into the woods, believing he was going to be picked up by aliens and succumbed to the elements, especially given the heavy storm that pummelled the area that night. Others point to the dynamite crater, the vehicle remains and the bone fragments as proof that Granger might simply have been the victim of a terrible accident.

In 1981, Granger's parents sold off the P-40 Kittyhawk fighter plane to a collector from Manitoba for $20,000. They deposited that money in Granger's account with the $10,000 that was already there in the hopes that Granger might someday return to use it. That hasn't happened, and it doesn't appear it ever will.

But even five years after Granger's disappearance, his parents appeared to be conflicted about whether or not they believed their son to be truly gone forever. One newspaper report describes the following, "His bed in his bedroom next to the kitchen is untouched. The plaques he saved from engines he'd repaired—triumphs and trophies of his mechanical aptitude—hang on a cupboard door."

Granger's stepfather Jim was reported in one newspaper story to have said the following about his son, "I can hardly believe Granger's off in a spaceship. But if there is a flying object out there, he's the one to find it."

The Mad Trapper of Rat River

~

I n late 1931, a mysterious man came to the attention of the RCMP in Aklavik in the Northwest Territories. He was first spotted by the police the previous summer when he arrived in Fort McPherson and was described as quiet, possibly Scandinavian and well equipped for living in the north.

That December, a Native trapper complained to the RCMP about someone messing with his traps and identified a man living nearby as the likely suspect. The man had a cabin on the Rat River, which the RCMP attended. The man inside, however, refused to speak to them, and when they tried to peek in one of his windows, the man inside covered it. RCMP Constable Alfred King and Special Constable Joe Bernard returned to Aklavik, obtained a search warrant and returned five days later with two other men. The man inside again refused to speak to them, and when the RCMP tried to force their way in, the man inside opened fire through the door. King was wounded and returned to Aklavik.

The RCMP formed a posse of nine men and returned to the cabin. They decided to use dynamite to blow their way into the cabin, but after the explosion, the man inside again opened fire; he was in a dugout underneath the cabin. The posse again retreated to get more reinforcements and returned on January 14 only to find the man had left. They pursued him and eventually surrounded him, but the man opened fire again, this time killing Constable Edgar Millen.

Again beaten back, the RCMP looked to famed bush pilot Wop May to help them find the man from the air, which he did using a ski-equipped plane. May was able to direct the team towards where the man was hiding on February 17. Another officer was shot in the ensuing confrontation, but this time the man was shot and killed.

Through all of the activity, no one had any idea who the man was. For the longest time people thought his name might be Arthur Nelson. It was later determined that his name was Albert Johnson. His remains were exhumed in 2009 and tested by a forensics team. They were able to determine that he was either from the United States or from Scandinavia, and that he had been approximately 30 years old when he died. Where he really came from and why he ran from the RCMP remains a mystery

Chapter 5

Oak Island

~

The promise and lure of buried treasure has captured the imagination of many. Whether it is rumours of a fortune in currency and jewels being plundered by bands of pirates and secreted away in some great hiding place or the lore of a vast fortune buried somewhere for safekeeping, many people have engaged in the business of treasure hunting. Secret caches of riches, however, have proven difficult for even the most ardent treasure hunters to find. And yet, despite lack of success, people will still dedicate a great deal of time and money to tracking down missing, lost or buried treasure.

There is one particular place in Canada on which dozens of treasure hunters have descended, even though little of any value has ever been recovered. In the more than 200 years since the rumours of buried treasure surfaced, scores of people have come to Oak Island, investing millions in excavating various parts of the island. But no treasure has ever been found or even proven to exist there. The search for treasure has claimed a half-dozen lives, but still people persist in searching. Backers of various digs have included some prominent people such as United States' President Franklin Roosevelt and even famous actor John Wayne.

Exactly what lies deep below the earth on this 57-hectare island off the coast of Nova Scotia—if anything does at all—is unclear. The stories of exactly what various crews have encountered as they dug their way down are so varied, and at times fantastical, that it is difficult to separate truth from legend. From a water source that floods tunnels that is either part of the natural formation of the island or was deliberately manipulated as a booby trap to protect whatever has been buried below, to stories of a stone with ancient markings that has since disappeared, the many lesser stories make up the greater history of the island and its fabled treasure and certainly make for an entertaining read. Despite the lack of any real evidence, theories abound about exactly who buried treasure on the island. These

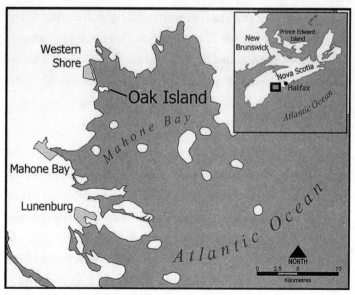

Location of Oak Island off the coast of Nova Scotia

theories include the great pirate Captain William Kidd stashing his booty on the island, French soldiers hiding the jewels of Marie Antoinette after the French Revolution or Sir Francis Bacon hiding evidence that he was the one who wrote William Shakespeare's plays. Even more theories prevail despite the fact nothing of any verified significance has ever been found on the island. And now that the island has become the subject of a reality television series, following a group of treasure hunters as they attempt to recover whatever treasure might be buried there, the island has now reached the status of legend.

Oak Island is a 57-hectare (140-acre) island in Lunenburg County on the south shore of Nova Scotia. It is one of approximately 360 small islands in Mahone Bay. The island rises to a maximum of 11 metres above sea level. It is roughly 200 metres from shore and is connected to the mainland. Despite its historical significance, the island is not a public park. It is privately owned, and the owners are intent on finding whatever treasure they believe to be buried out there.

The history of the island and its treasure hunting starts in 1795. It is generally accepted that an 18-year-old man named Daniel McGinnis noticed some lights coming from the island. He decided to investigate. When he reached the island, he found a clearing on the southeastern end of the island where the ground looked a little strange. It was slightly depressed, and the resulting depression formed the shape of a circle. It looked as if someone had been digging in the area. As McGinnis looked around, he noticed a few other things that stood out.

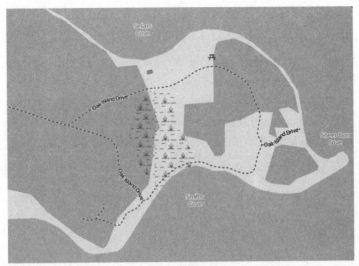

Map of Oak Island. Shows the swamp near the centre right. Smith's Cove is at the bottom of the island.

~

Near the depression stood a tree that had branches projecting out over the depression, and the bark on the branches was marked by a series of cuts, as if it a rope had been thrown over it to help lift or lower something. A block and tackle was also found nearby.

McGinnis had heard stories of pirates in the area and quickly came to the conclusion that someone had been digging there. He decided to see what might be below the surface of the depression. He returned to the island and started digging. He was accompanied by friends, Anthony Vaughan and either John Smith or Samuel Ball, depending on the account. During their first round, the group dug down about nine metres, but what they found made them even more curious about what might be below. At a depth of half a metre, they came across a layer of flagstones. Digging down another two and a half metres, they encountered a layer of oak logs. They found a second layer of logs somewhere between eight and nine metres. As they dug, they also came across markings on the dirt and rock walls of the shaft that looked as if they might have come from a pick.

The group stopped its search, but returned again approximately eight years later. They formed the Onslow Company to facilitate digging on the island and picked up where they had left off eight years earlier. As the workers dug down further, they kept coming across layers of oak logs about every three metres. At 12 metres, they encountered a layer of charcoal. At 15 metres was a layer of a putty-like substance. And at 18 metres came one

Money Pit at Oak Island

of the strangest findings to date—a layer of fibre that was later concluded to be coconut fibre. This was a particularly curious find, since coconuts are not native to Nova Scotia.

That find, however, was trumped by what they found at a depth of 27 metres. The diggers unearthed a strange stone. The stone bore an inscription of several strange, curious symbols. No one at the time could decipher what, if anything, these symbols represented. The group kept digging, but as they passed through 27 metres, the shaft began to flood. They tried to bail out the water, but their efforts proved ineffectual, and the shaft flooded all the way up to the 10-metre level. Frustrated but not broken, the group returned the following year with a new plan. They would dig a new pit parallel to the original, which became known as the Money Pit, then tunnel over to the Money Pit. They made it down to a depth of approximately 100 metres before the new shaft also flooded. This last setback was all the members of the Onslow Company could withstand. They pulled out and left. So Oak Island and the mystery below its surface would be abandoned again, this time for about 45 years.

News of what was taking place at Oak Island circulated in North America, and in 1849, a new group came along to try its hand at unearthing whatever might be buried on the island. The Truro Company started digging, but only got as far down as 26 metres before the entire pit again flooded. Rather than try to dig a separate shaft, the group decided instead to start drilling down to take core samples to see what they found. At 30 metres, the drill passed through what was determined to be a spruce platform. As the drill continued past the spruce platform, it passed through 10 centimetres of oak, 55 centimetres of pieces of metal, then another 10 centimetres of oak and another layer of spruce. When the drill was finally removed, the crew found splinters of oak and strands of what they believe to be coconut husks. One account of this drilling has the crews also recovering three small gold links, as if from a chain, but this account has never been verified, and the links themselves haven't been seen since, if they were recovered at all.

The combinations of materials in the core samples—the oak, the metal pieces, followed by more oak—led the drillers to believe they had drilled through two casks or chests filled with coins. They even found in these samples that the earth beneath the first spruce platform was loose and less compacted, as if it had been dug up once before. Buoyed by their results, the Truro Company returned a year later to dig a new shaft, this one again parallel to the Money Pit, with the intent of tunnelling over. But the new shaft also flooded. The company tried pumping the water out of the pit, but this proved to be an ineffective way of dealing with the water, and they were forced to abandon the shaft.

It was this episode of pumping that led searchers to believe that the Money Pit was deliberately booby-trapped to flood if anyone drilled down far enough. Some have argued that the Truro Company actually discovered that the beach at Smith's Cove, where they were pumping, was actually an artificial beach that was part of an elaborate booby-trap to protect whatever might be buried in the Money Pit. Those who put stock in the story believe the designers of the original Money Pit built a drain system in the form of a 44-metre length of beach, resembling the fingers of a hand. Each of those "fingers" is a channel dug into the clay under the beach, and each channel is lined with materials such as rock, grass and coconut fibre. These channels then meet at a point inland where they feed sea water into a main channel that joins up with the Money Pit. It is this channel that causes the Money Pit to flood at depths of 28 to 30 metres The channel was found to be approximately one metre wide and three-quarters of a metre high and lined with limestone. As a result of its findings, Truro Company is alleged to have attempted to divert the channel by building a dam just off the beach before trying to dismantle these channels, but the dam was destroyed in a storm. They also tried to dig a pit 30 metres inland to meet the water channel and plug it, but this undertaking failed as well. It proved to be Truro's last attempt to excavate on the island.

The next group of treasure hunters only waited 12 years before descending on the island. This time the group was called the Oak Island Association. The group decided to tackle the Money Pit head on, digging to a depth of 27 metres. It also worked on a new hole east of the pit in the hopes of intercepting whatever channel was causing the flooding. They never found the channel, so the hole was abandoned. They tried digging another shaft west of the Money Pit. They made it down to 36 metres intending to tunnel over to the Money Pit. But again water started to seep into the Money Pit. The workers started to bail, with some success when, without warning, the bottom of the Money Pit dropped four and a half metres. The episode fuelled the belief that the pit was booby-trapped, although some simply argued that the excavation crews had encountered a natural cavern beneath the pit. While no one was injured in the collapse of the pit, it was the Oak Island Association that would count the first of what would become six fatalities in the history of the island. A boiler on one of the pumping engines burst, killing one worker. Finally, in 1865, the Oak Island Association ran out of money and was forced to stop digging.

In 1893, the Oak Island Treasure Company formed and decided to try a new search. This group believed that there was a second pit on the island—106 metres east of the Money Pit—that had been dug by the designers of the original Money Pit for ventilation while digging the flood channel. This pit, however, flooded when crews reached a depth of 17 metres. They tried

Aerial photo of the digs and buildings around the Money Pit, August 1931

pumping and digging other shafts to no avail. In 1897 they went to work on the Money Pit, even going so far as to try dynamiting the suspected flood tunnels, again to no effect. The group drilled for more core samples and, according to some accounts, the crew got down to 38 metres where it struck wood, then iron, both of which were believed to be part of the material that fell when the bottom collapsed earlier. Core samples from 39 metres and 46 metres as well as 48 and 51 metres turned up a blue type of clay that could have been the putty found during the earliest digs. Between those layers of putty, the story goes, was material that led the workers to believe they had come across a cement vault. The vault appeared to be two metres high with walls four-centimetres thick. Inside the vault, the drill retrieved samples of wood, an unknown substance, soft metal, approximately one-metre of metal pieces, then more soft metal. When the drill was brought up, so the story goes, a small piece of sheepskin parchment was attached to it. The parchment bore the letters "vi," "ui" and "wi," but no one knew what to make of the find. More shafts were then dug as a result of the find, but they also flooded.

More companies made attempts at the Money Pit in the early 20th century but found little of any note. One company, however, went on to have some famous backing. The Old Gold Salvage Group, which did some excavating work in 1909, had Franklin Roosevelt as one of its partners. It's said that Roosevelt actually kept up with news about Oak Island and the various digs taking place on it for most of his life afterwards.

Other excavations occurred over the years, but little of any real importance was found. To try to solve part of the mystery of the flooding in most of the shafts dug to date, one crew tried pouring red paint into the flooded pit. Doing so helped highlight three different exit holes around the island through which the water flowed.

But someone was putting a lot of thought into how to solve the mystery of Oak Island. Numerous publications dating back to the 1860s mentioned Oak Island and the various excavations taking place there. In 1928, one New York newspaper published a feature story on the island's history. That story caught the attention of one Gilbert Hedden. Hedden owned a business that manufactured steel, but he was captivated by the problems that the crews on Oak Island had encountered. Specifically the engineering required to dig down to the island's purported treasure captivated his attention. Hedden read as much as he could about the island and started making trips there. He even went so far as to travel to England to have a long chat with Harold T. Wilkins. Wilkins was the author of the book *Captain Kidd and His Skeleton Island*. Hedden thought that there might be a connection between the island and one of the maps featured in Wilkins' book. Hedden eventually purchased a few parcels of land on the island and began digging.

Some artifacts had emerged in other searches. William Chappel had been digging on the island since 1934 and had successfully excavated a 50-metre-deep shaft. At 39 metres he came across several artifacts—an axe, an anchor fluke and a pick. The pick was identified as a Cornish miner's poll pick. The find, however, was viewed sceptically because of all the debris in the area. It made authenticating the find difficult.

Suddenly there was renewed interest in the stone with the strange inscriptions that had been found. In 1951, a book written by Edward Rowe Snow was published entitled *True Tales of Buried Treasure*. In the book, Snow included a reproduction of the symbols on the stone along with a translation even though the stone itself hadn't been seen since earlier in the 20th century. He said that Reverend A.T. Kempton of Cambridge, Massachusetts, gave him the translation of the symbols, but little was known about Kempton and his involvement in the Oak Island mystery.

The translation read as follows:

40 feet below, two million pounds lie buried.

But Kempton's wasn't the only translation. A copy of the markings was also sent to a fellow named Barry Fell who had written a book in which he translated markings on stone. He said the symbols resembled the Coptic alphabet. According to Fell, the symbols stated that people needed to worship God or they would die.

But the first translation fuelled the belief that *something* was buried below the surface of the island and the treasure hunting continued. In 1959, Bob Restall and his family started working on the island. They came across a rock with the number 1704 written on it. The rock was later dismissed, however, as a prank, left behind by a previous search team. Unfortunately, Restall's search ended tragically. One day in 1965, while working at the bottom of a shaft he was excavating, Bob passed out and fell into the water at the bottom of the shaft. His son Bobbie and two workers descended into the shaft to help him, but in the process the three would-be rescuers were overcome by exhaust from a generator being used in the excavation. All of them passed out from the fumes and drowned.

That same year, another excavator decided to get serious about his treasure hunting, and in so doing helped connect Oak Island to the rest of Nova Scotia. Bob Dunfield decided it was time to bring in heavy machinery to work on the excavation, machines such as bulldozers and cranes. To get the machinery to the island, a causeway was built, and it still exists to this day. One crane was a 63.5-tonne digging crane that was able to dig down to a depth of 41 metres. However, despite the fact that crews carefully sifted through large quantities of soil, nothing of any value was recovered.

Eventually, one of the largest island landowners started getting to work as well. By 1971, most of the island had been bought by Triton Alliance, formed by Daniel Blankenship and David Tobias. Triton crews were able to dig down some 71 metres into the island, and they lowered video cameras into the cavity at the bottom of the shaft. Many interpretations have been given of exactly what images those video cameras were able to capture. Blankenship and Tobias maintained that the footage showed such features as human bodies, chests (as in treasure chests), tools and even wooden cribbing. Other accounts said the footage clearly showed three treasure chests and a severed human hand. Some say that divers were sent down into the shaft but because of a strong current and poor visibility, they were unable to see anything.

The shaft apparently also produced other finds, although their authenticity has never been verified. In digging through the shaft, some maintain Triton found several logs that were six centimetres thick and up to 19 metres long. These logs were marked every 1.2 metres with Roman numerals. Some of the logs were even said to contain wooden pins or nails. Another account claims that the wood in the logs was carbon-dated to 250 years earlier.

Unfortunately, the shaft collapsed again. It was later dug again to a depth of 17 metres, reaching bedrock, but Triton, like so many other groups before it, ran out of money. So they were forced to abandon their search.

Soon the notoriety of the island became much more public. *Reader's Digest* published a story about Oak Island and its elusive treasure in 1965. In January 1979, Oak Island went mainstream when it was featured in an episode of *In Search Of....* Putting Oak Island on television revealed its history to more and more people.

Drilling, however, ground to a halt for most of the 1980s and 1990s because of legal battles among the Triton partners. During that time, some crews decided to actually go and evaluate the island's underground water sources from a scientific perspective by running dye tests in the borehole—they put dye in the hole and then observed where the coloured water emerged from around the island. As a result, the crews were able to determine that the flooding was a natural result of tidal pressures surrounding the island, as well as its own freshwater lens—an area where rainwater seeps through soil and gathers over a layer of seawater. Scientists even went so far as to scrutinise the videos made in the 1970s when video cameras were lowered into the large underground cavity at the bottom of the Triton shaft. They concluded that nothing definitive could be determined from the video.

David Tobias eventually sold his share of the island to a group from Michigan in 2006. Blankenship announced a year later that he and his new partners were ready to start pumping more money into excavating the island. They even wanted to carbon-date some of the material found near the area of the shaft dug in the '70s, which is known as Borehole 10-X. One of the new partners went so far as to say that he believed the island was hiding gold and silver from the Inca or Mayan empires that was taken by the Spanish or British when they raided those empires centuries earlier.

"If I didn't think there was something on the island, I wouldn't be here," Blankenship told the *National Post* in 2010. "And I sure as hell didn't stay here for 40 years thinking there was nothing."

In that time, Oak Island has continued to be a source of inspiration in popular culture. More than 50 books have been published on the island's history, with varying theories as to what could possibly be buried there. Several works of fiction have also been written centring on the island and its notoriety.

The island was also featured in the popular video game *Assassin's Creed III* where a player gets to island by completing quests related to Captain Kidd. It has also been featured on the documentary TV series *Northern Mysteries* and in an episode of the TV series *Bones*, entitled "The Man with the Bone."

But the most exposure Oak Island has seen has been the result of a reality TV show called *The Curse of Oak Island* launched in January 2014. The show features brothers Marty and Rick Lagina, treasure hunters on the island. At times episodes of the show have ranked as the most watched cable TV program on the nights that they air. The final episode of the first season showed the brothers finding what they believed to be a Spanish coin from the 1600s. The second season finale, however, was much more dramatic. Crews had successfully dug down to the mysterious cavern located at a depth of approximately 72 metres. They lowered a scanning sonar device into the cavern to produce a picture of what was inside. The scan revealed the chamber to be rectangular in shape, containing several large rectangular objects. Some of those objects were interpreted as being human made.

Numerous theories have emerged about what may be buried beneath the earth of Oak Island. One of the most notable theories is that what is buried below Oak Island is honest-to-goodness pirate treasure, left there by one of two pirates—either Captain Kidd or the infamous Blackbeard (Edward Teach).

Captain William Kidd, born in Scotland, lived from 1645 to 1701. He was tried for piracy and subsequently executed.

Some believe that Kidd buried several caches of treasure on Oak Island. If Kidd was actually a pirate, then there is a possibility he did so. But there is some debate in historical circles about whether Kidd was an actual pirate or a privateer (a private sailor authorized by the British government to attack ships belonging to foreign governments), who was unfairly accused of and tried for piracy then executed as a result. Historical records indicate that Kidd did stash some treasure in his travels at various locations, which has helped fuel the belief that he may have buried some of it on Oak Island.

In Teach's case, there is no doubt that he was a pirate. He was killed in a battle trying to avoid capture. As for whether or not Teach buried anything of value, the only treasure recovered that has been definitively linked to him was recovered from his ship, which was found and excavated in 1997.

Another popular theory is that British or Spanish sailors may have buried treasure on the island. In the case of the Spanish, the treasure is believed to be the spoils of raids on the Incan and Mayan empires. Others contend it may have been left there by sailors on board a Spanish galleon who had originally found the treasure in a wrecked ship that had become stranded on or near the island. As for the British, some contend that the British buried treasure there during the American Revolution.

Others implicate the French. Adherents to this theory believe that the complexity of the Money Pit means that French army engineers buried treasure there. Following this theory, the supposed treasure could have come from one of two sources.

The first is that it could have been moved there from the fortress at Louisbourg before it fell to the British in 1758. A variation on this theory suggests that the pit may have been built by the French as a decoy to protect the real Louisbourg treasure from being found. This theory points to such features of the pit as the block and tackle found hanging from a tree, the stone with the strange markings and the fact the pit flooded at a deeper depth than where the stone was found. These elements convinced treasure hunters something is there to be found when, in fact, there may be nothing.

A second theory involving the French states that the treasure buried on Oak Island is jewels belonging to Marie Antoinette, wife of former King Louis XVI of France. The story goes that as her palace was being stormed in 1789 during the French Revolution, Antoinette ordered either a maid or another servant to take her jewels, as well as some documents and artwork and flee. That person somehow made their way to London. They then somehow travelled from London to Nova Scotia and also somehow contracted the French Navy to build the pit on the island to bury the valuables.

Another theory, proposed in the 1953 book *The Oak Island Enigma: A History and Inquiry in the Origin of the Money Pit*, states that the pit was built to hide manuscripts showing that it was actually Sir Francis Bacon who wrote the works traditionally attributed to William Shakespeare. Other books have stated there are clues within the works that Shakespeare wrote indicating that it was actually Bacon who wrote them.

Yet another theory involves the Knights Templar, a western Christian military order that served during the Crusades and became one of the most powerful groups of its time. The order was later devastated when it was disbanded and persecuted. Some contend that the Knights Templar used Oak Island to hide nothing less than the Ark of the Covenant, the chest that, according to the Book of Exodus, holds the stone tablets on which the Ten Commandments were originally written. The same theory also holds that a Templar grave may also be on the island. Intertwined with this theory is a legend of unknown origin that states that seven people must die before the treasure can be uncovered. Theorists point to the fact that six people have died so far trying to unearth the treasure.

Some also think that other markings found on Oak Island, as well as in the pit, are proof the island is associated with a Masonic initiation rite involving a hidden vault containing a buried treasure. It has been argued that many of the excavators who have worked on the island have had ties to the Freemasons.

Others believe the items found are parts of a Viking ship that sank and somehow settled on the island in a vertical position and that there is no treasure on the island other than the ship itself and any artifacts that might have come from it. This theory could explain the layers of logs, as well as the fibres such as coconut fibre, which could have been used for backrests, pillows or mattresses.

More realistic theories contend that whatever is below the surface is natural in origin. They say that the cavern is a natural sinkhole or some other phenomenon linked to a series of passages, and that the wood could have simply been drift-wood or fallen trees that washed up on shore hundreds of years earlier. One note in the history of Oak Island does state that it was scientists at the Smithsonian Museum that identified the fibre found on the island as coconut fibre, and that identification was made at some point in the early 20th century. If true, the coconut fibre would be intriguing for the simple fact that coconut trees are not native to Oak Island, or any part of Canada for that matter, so the presence of that fibre could not be easily explained.

And so the mystery remains. How any group of individuals three hundred years ago could build a pit so deep and so booby-trapped, with the tools and knowledge they had available to them at the time that no person in modern time can possibly overcome with modern tools and technology is unclear. But so long as there are believers in the legends of the island, the search for buried treasure will no doubt continue on Oak Island.

Lost Lemon Mine

~

There are more rumours of buried treasure, outside of the Money Pit on Oak Island. And one those legendary stories is of a gold mine allegedly located in Alberta that, if found, would make its finder instantly wealthy.

The mine in question is the Lost Lemon Mine, named for one of the men credited with finding it in the Crowsnest Pass in the late 1800s. The story goes that, sometime in the 1870s, two prospectors from the United States, one named Lemon, the other named Blackjack, came up to Canada looking for gold. They began their search around the North Saskatchewan River. Apparently, the two men found signs of gold and, in tracing the gold to its source, came upon an area that was thick with gold. However, as is often the case in situations involving money, a disagreement ensued between the two men over whether or not they should start mining immediately or return in the spring. After the two went to sleep that night, Lemon killed Blackjack, splitting his head open with an axe. Lemon was distraught over what he had done.

The legend also says that a nearby group of Blackfoot witnessed the murder and, when they told their chief what had happened, the chief put a curse on the area. The curse has been credited with the deaths of two prospectors who came looking for the lost mine. One was a trapper who drank himself to death looking for the mine, and the other a prospector whose cabin caught fire with him inside it. Lemon himself either forgot the location or simply never bothered to look for it ever again.

Many people have searched for the mine since then, but while some gold has been found in the area, it has not been in high enough concentration to be economically worthwhile to mine. The Lost Lemon Mine is still eluding searchers to this day—truly lost.

Chapter 6
E. Herbert Norman

~

Oone of the worst things you could be in the 1950s in Canada and the United States was a Communist. It was equally criminal to even be suspected of being a Communist or to have once been a Communist. Accusations of participation in socialist groups, coupled with the philosophical impossibility of proving a negative, such as that one was not a Communist, ruined careers and lives across North America during the Cold War.

Canada was not immune to the Red Scare. The government had taken the highly provocative step in September 1939, when war was declared against Germany, of rounding up all the Communist leaders and holding them. While the Canadian government did not stoop to the level of the United States with its witch-hunts of Communists, described by Minister of External Affairs Lester B. Pearson as "the black madness of the witch-hunt," it still took steps to check into the political sympathies of citizens, public servants and other prominent individuals. Security checks were stepped up—70,000 checks were done in one year alone. The province of Québec even passed a law giving police the power to seal any building where communist activity was suspected of taking place.

It was in this atmosphere of oppression in April 1957, that the government of Canada received startling news. Its ambassador to Egypt, who had been integral in defusing the Suez Crisis months earlier, had leapt to his death from the seventh floor of a building in Cairo. His name was Egerton Herbert Norman, a long-serving member of the External Affairs branch, former ambassador to New Zealand and once an advisor to General Douglas MacArthur, the Supreme Allied Commander of occupied Japan at the conclusion of World War II. He left behind his wife Irene.

In the days that followed, Canadian politicians placed the blame for Norman's suicide at the feet of the United States of America. Norman's name had again come up in the communist witch-hunt that was the Senate Internal Security Sub-Committee in Washington, D.C. Indeed one MP stated that Norman had been murdered "by slander." It was not the first time Norman's name had come up at the committee. Yet despite repeated attempts by External Affairs to protect Norman and even one RCMP report that exonerated him, some in the United States government were convinced that Norman was both a Communist and a spy. They were determined to bring him down.

In a note that was found after Norman's death, he intimated it was the ongoing pursuit by the U.S. government that made him decide to jump to his death.

In one of the two letters he left behind, he wrote:

The forces against me are too formidable, even for an inno-cent man and it is better to go now than to live indefinitely pelted with mud.

However, in the ensuing years, more mystery than clar-ity has surrounded Norman and his death. Was he really a com-munist? Was he a spy or an agent of influence for the Soviet Union? Why would such a talented civil servant commit suicide during a time of great personal triumph? Had he committed suicide for the reasons given, or did he do so to hide the fact that he was actually a Communist spy?

~

Herbert Norman's service to his country was perhaps more notable because of the fact he was neither born nor raised in Canada. He was born in 1909 in Karuizawa, Japan. His father, Daniel, had gone to Japan in 1902 as a Methodist mis-sionary, accompanied by his wife. Norman had one brother and one sister. He spent his entire childhood in Japan, often accom-panying his father on his missionary work. Norman was exposed to communism at an early age. His father worked with farmers and rail workers in Japan, as well as with a fledgling reform movement. Daniel often remarked that Jesus himself had taught some communism.

When at age 18, Norman contracted tuberculosis, he was sent to a sanatorium in Canada—Calgary, in fact—to recover. He was there for one year before striking off to pursue his post-secondary education. He first enrolled at Victoria

Egerton Herbert Norman as a youth

~

College at the University of Toronto, studying honours classics. As Norman began his studies, the world around him was reeling as the stock market crashed, and millions across North America were plunged into unemployment and poverty. Both within the intellectual confines of post-secondary institutions as well as in the line-ups outside soup kitchens, dissatisfaction with capitalism was growing and the most affected were looking to the political ideology of communism as a potential solution to the world's problems. Norman was not an active participant or member of any party; he was more of an intellectual communist, someone who appreciated the ideology but not someone who would necessarily act upon it.

In 1933, Norman travelled overseas to study at Cambridge, in a move that would later catch the attention of the anti-communist movement in the United States. In the 1930s, Cambridge was fertile ground for communism to take root and grow. Some notorious figures came out of Cambridge, such as Kim Philby, Guy Burgess, Donald MacLean and Anthony Blunt, all of whom were later revealed as Soviet spies. But in the 1930s, they were students and Communists. Norman walked in the same circle as this infamous group; he joined one Communist cell in Cambridge that opposed the spread of fascism in Europe. Benito Mussolini was in power in Italy, and Adolf Hitler's rise to power was well underway. For those leaning towards communism, the growing conflicts and depression of the 1930s were proof that capitalism had failed and that the rest of the world was fertile ground from which communism could bloom worldwide. Norman befriended several other Communists at Cambridge, and the university also assigned him to work with visiting students from India.

Once he finished his studies at Cambridge, Norman headed back to North America, but not to Canada. He received a prestigious Rockefeller Foundation Fellowship to study Japanese history at Harvard. At the time, he was courting Irene Clark, whom he had met at Victoria College. They eventually married.

The Communists of the world were up in arms as Hitler and Mussolini tightened their grips on power, but there was a new face on Fascism. Francisco Franco was on the march in Spain, and the Communists of the world held up the plight of the people of Spain as a call to arms. Communists from all over the world flocked to Spain to bolster the anti-Franco side of the civil war. Several of Norman's friends from Cambridge made the trip to fight Franco, and Norman himself gave some thought to going as well. He concluded, however, that he did not have the required skills to be a good fighter and chose to remain in the U.S. Norman continued to support communism in general. He became the secretary of a group that supported communism in China and joined the League Against War and Fascism, an organization dominated by Communists. He also joined a Marxist study group at Harvard. Alongside his studies, Norman began writing his first book, entitled *Japan's Emergence As A Modern State*, a book that would eventually land Norman some important work overseas.

But for now, Norman finished his studies at Harvard, finished his book and applied for a job with the Department of External Affairs in Canada. He was hired as a Japanese Language Officer and joined a group of young, educated intellectuals who played a role in shaping Canada's foreign policy. It was no surprise that more than a few of those working in the department would later be identified as Communists. Norman also began working with an External Affairs employee whose career would become closely tied to Norman's. His name was Lester Bowles Pearson.

Canada was relatively new at handling its own foreign policy. Great Britain granted Canada control of its own foreign affairs in 1909, and Canada was still working to expand its influence. Because the department was so new, relatively few security protocols were in place. Consequently, Norman and others with similar beliefs were never subjected to any kind of security or background check. It's not that he would have been unwelcome. Prime Minister William Lyon Mackenzie-King was once quoted as saying he "didn't mind having a few communists around." But even though no one seemed to care from a security perspective about the beliefs of those in the department, Norman recognized that some of his past associations might come back to haunt him. The outbreak of World War II was bad news for communists in North America; many leaders were rounded up and interred. Norman subsequently began distancing himself from his communist friends in an effort to protect his career, which was about to take off.

With the release of his book, Norman became one of the foremost authorities in the western hemisphere on Japan, and that distinction couldn't have come at a more important time. Japan was looking beyond its own borders, having invaded and conquered Manchuria in 1931 and invaded China in 1937. In September 1940, Japan signed an alliance with Germany and Italy, a move the Allies viewed with great suspicion. Norman, now a rising star in External Affairs, was dispatched to the country where he'd been raised, serving as Third Secretary of the Canadian legation in Japan. It was a sobering experience. His parents, who were still living in Japan, were constantly interrogated by the Japanese authorities. Many left-wing scholars, especially Communists, were jailed or went into hiding.

On December 7, 1941, Japan launched a surprise attack against Pearl Harbour, killing more than 2500 Americans, destroying 18 ships of the United States Navy as well as 300 airplanes. Back in Japan, the authorities moved against foreign legations, placing Norman and those he worked with under house arrest. He stayed there for seven months before he was exchanged for several Japanese individuals that were being deported from the United States. One of those was Norman's friend, Shigeto Tsuru, whom he had met at Harvard. In passing, Tsuru mentioned to Norman that Norman could have Tsuru's collection of books on Japanese history, which were back at his apartment in the United States. When he got back home, Norman took Tsuru up on his offer and headed to the apartment. But he was not the only one interested in the contents of Tsuru's apartment. When Norman arrived, he was confronted by a team of FBI agents. The FBI had found out about the Marxist study group at Harvard and were searching Tsuru's apartment. When they started to ask Norman questions, Norman replied that he had come to the apartment on official business of the Canadian government. The FBI, however, was suspicious, and as a result of that encounter, they opened a file on Herbert Norman. When he returned to Canada, Norman told Pearson what had happened, and Pearson dispatched a letter to J. Edgar Hoover, the head of the FBI. Hoover never replied.

In August 1945, Japan surrendered to the Allies. Ten days later, Norman headed back to Japan, but not as a member of a Canadian legation. The United States State Department had persuaded Canada's External Affairs department to allow them to second Norman to the American Counter-Intelligence Corps. In this role, he became a close confidant of General

Douglas MacArthur, head of the occupation forces in Japan. Part of his job was to arrange for the release of imprisoned Japanese radicals who had opposed the war. Many Communists were in that group. After discussing it further with MacArthur, it was decided that Norman would travel to Fuchu Prison to release the political prisoners being held there, many of whom had been imprisoned for as long as 19 years.

AMERICANS.....
DON'T PATRONIZE REDS!!!!

————•————

YOU CAN DRIVE THE REDS OUT OF TELEVISION, RADIO AND HOLLY-WOOD.....

THIS TRACT WILL TELL YOU HOW.

WHY WE MUST DRIVE THEM OUT:

1) The REDS have made our Screen, Radio and TV Moscow's most effective Fifth Column in America . . . 2) The REDS of Hollywood and Broadway have always been the chief financial support of Communist propaganda in America . . . 3) OUR OWN FILMS, made by RED Producers, Directors, Writers and STARS, are being used by Moscow in ASIA, Africa, the Balkans and throughout Europe to create hatred of America . . . 4) RIGHT NOW films are being made to craftily glorify MARXISM, UNESCO and ONE-WORLDISM . . . and via your TV Set they are being piped into your Living Room—and are poisoning the minds of your children under your very eyes ! ! !

So REMEMBER — If you patronize a Film made by RED Producers, Writers, Stars and STUDIOS you are aiding and abetting COMMUNISM . . . every time you permit REDS to come into your Living Room VIA YOUR TV SET you are helping MOSCOW and the INTERNATIONALISTS to destroy America ! ! !

U.S. anti-Communist literature of the 1950s, specifically aimed at the entertainment industry

It was this prisoner release, even though it came with the blessing of General MacArthur, that would reignite the FBI's investigation into reports that Norman was a Communist. MacArthur's second-in-command, Brigadier General Charles Willoughby, a hardened anti-communist was harshly critical of the release of the prisoners. Thanks to Willoughby's criticism, the FBI reopened its file on Norman.

When his secondment expired, Norman was named head of the Canadian legation to Japan. At only 37 years of age, the appointment was a great honour for Norman. Because of his service to the Occupation Government, he maintained a good relationship with MacArthur. But the United States' initial enthusiasm to create a Japan completely free for all was starting to wane. The communist movement in China, under Mao Zedong was on the rise, and the United States was nervous about its possible spread throughout Asia. The U.S. government ordered MacArthur to reverse course. Communist leaders were rearrested, while popular labour leaders were fired from their jobs. To register his disapproval, Norman took the rare step, during a public speech, of criticizing the American government's change in policy. Diplomats were expected to keep their opinions to themselves, and Norman's criticism only gave Willoughby more ammunition to pursue the investigation into Norman's background. Willoughby became even more suspicious because Norman's friend Tsuru was now working with the Japanese government. It looked to Willoughby as if the two were working together in order to further the cause of communism in Japan. Norman tried to ignore Willoughby's issues, pursuing his career in External Affairs and even writing a second book.

But when the Soviet Union detonated its first nuclear bomb in 1949, the Cold War, which had been brewing since the end of World War II, was officially underway. As a result, anyone who had anything to do with communist ideology at any time in their lives was now being treated with heavy suspicion in the United States. The House Committee on Un-American Activities and the Senate Internal Security Subcommittee (SISS) were accusing anyone they could find of being a Communist. So it was inevitable, given the FBI's interest in him, that Herbert Norman's name eventually came to light, first in the SISS, on April 20, 1950. Hoover passed Norman's file to the committee, and the committee heard from a witness that Norman's release of prisoners after the war had revitalized the communist movement in Japan. What the committee did *not* hear was that MacArthur had ordered Norman to release those prisoners. The committee also heard that Norman's contacts with the left-wing movements in Japan were part of an evil plot, but the committee did not hear that Norman had actually been working with the occupation government at the time.

The day after his name first came up at SISS, the Department of External Affairs heard about it, but they chose to do little at first. Lester Pearson was convinced that the brewing controversy over Norman would just blow over. Consequently, the department did not issue a statement about Norman. But despite a lack of solid evidence that Norman had done anything wrong, he was still seen as an enemy by many in the United States government.

J. Edgar Hoover, Director of the Federal Bureau of Investigation in the U.S. from 1924 to 1972

~

Other circumstances were coalescing to make life even more difficult for Norman. The RCMP had arrested Israel Halperin on espionage charges in large part as a result of information gleaned from Soviet defector Igor Gouzenko. Halperin and Norman had roomed together at Victoria College, and Norman's name had been found in one Halperin's notebooks. A British scientist also arrested on espionage charges also had his name in Halperin's notebook, but Norman had never met the man. While the RCMP initially declined to investigate the connection, the FBI ran with it, forcing the RCMP to eventually open its own file on Norman.

As a result, Norman was ordered back to Ottawa, namely because Pearson wanted to give Norman the chance to speak. Pearson asked to see the RCMP file before they sent it to the FBI, but the request came too late. The file had already been sent to Washington. On October 21, 1950, the RCMP interrogated Norman. New security rules passed by the government made membership in any Communist Party cause for dismissal. Under questioning, Norman admitted only to being associated with different "radical undergraduate groups," and he stated that while he was friends with some who had communist beliefs, he did not know their political affiliations. The interrogation went on for weeks, and at one point Norman broke down in tears. After six weeks, the RCMP concluded that there was no evidence of espionage and that Norman hadn't betrayed his country.

The report read: "He has frequently failed to properly assess his social acquaintances but rather accepted at their face value all those who interested him without being conscious of their ideologies." The report concluded that Norman did show some sympathies towards communism.

"By the time he entered Harvard, he advises he had come to the conclusion that communism was not the answer to the world's problems," the report said, but that is all they could find.

"We are of the opinion that NORMAN was never developed, consciously or unconsciously, by the Russians," the report said. Furthermore, "There has been no evidence uncovered which would indicate disloyalty on the part of NORMAN. The worst possible conclusion we can arrive at is the very apparent naïveté in his relationship with his fellow man."

The FBI didn't believe the RCMP, but there was little else they could do. In a move that further upset the U.S., Norman was assigned as head of the American and Far Eastern Division at External Affairs, which gave him access to classified information. As a result, the Americans refused to deal with him.

In May 1951, Guy Burgess and Donald MacLean, who had been students at Cambridge at the same time as Norman, defected to the Soviet Union, and in so doing were exposed as Soviet spies. Knowing that Norman had attended school with them, there were those in the U.S. who tried to find a link between Norman and the two defectors. Pearson defied the U.S. again when he appointed Norman as a delegate to the United Nations, which many in the U.S. government already believed was full of Communists. His name again started appearing at SISS. Robert Morris, counsel for the committee, was determined to find something to pin on Norman.

Another witness came forward to report that Norman was a Communist. The witness said he was part of the same Marxist study group that Norman had attended while studying at Harvard. His testimony was later released to the press. The move forced Pearson to respond publicly, saying that the RCMP had concluded its own investigation and found that Norman had done nothing wrong. But the U.S. government kept at it. Pearson's continued defence of Norman, as well as his push at the UN to recognize Communist China, prompted the FBI to open a file on Pearson. The growing furball of controversy prompted Norman to request Pearson relieve him of his post because he didn't want to be an embarrassment to Pearson and to Canada. Norman was called back to Ottawa where he was tasked with preparing a foreign policy survey.

But the British government was starting to pursue Norman as well. They confronted the RCMP with testimony from a high-ranking member of the British Communist Party who told them that Norman had been a member of the party during his days in Cambridge and that he had tried to use his position working with students from India to recruit them into the party. The RCMP responded by questioning Norman again in January 1952. Norman, ever the gentleman, refused to implicate anyone.

"I talked quite recklessly in those years, and I might have been a bit carefree and I didn't weigh my words," he told the RCMP. When his interrogators said they didn't believe he was innocent, Norman replied, "I am not aware that I have ever violated my duty to my government nor have I ever engaged in what you might call conspiratorial activities, trying to pass off secret messages and this sort of thing."

The RCMP concluded its interrogation. They told Pearson that Norman was a risk to the security of Canada and that he should be removed from public service. Pearson refused. He personally reviewed Norman's testimony and concluded that while he might have been a Communist at Cambridge, there was no proof he was ever a spy. Pearson ordered the RCMP to close their file, and he dispatched Norman to New Zealand as High Commissioner, hoping everyone would forget about him.

After three years, the Pearson wrongfully assumed that everyone had forgotten about Norman, and so Pearson appointed Norman as Canada's ambassador to Egypt. The appointment would prove controversial because of its timing. On July 26, 1956, while giving a speech in Alexandria, Egyptian President Gamal Nasser spoke the name Ferdinand de Lesspes, the builder of the Suez Canal. That name was a code word for Egyptian forces to seize the Suez Canal, which had been under the control of the Suez Canal Company, a joint Britain-France enterprise. Egypt's actions provoked the French and British, as well as the Israelis.

Norman arrived in Egypt to take his post three weeks after Egypt seized the canal. He met with Nasser shortly afterwards. Nasser told Norman he believed Canada was loyal to Britain, but also told Norman he felt Canada was sympathetic to nations that were emerging from colonial rule. It was an important moment for Norman, as he was able to develop a good relationship with Nasser that would prove beneficial as the crisis deepened.

On October 29, 1956, Israel invaded the Sinai Peninsula. It was a move that had been negotiated in advance among the countries of Britain, France and Israel. Britain and France issued an ultimatum for both sides to stop fighting, and five days later, both countries landed paratroopers along the canal. But Israel, Britain and France were missing one key element in their move against the Middle East, the blessing of the United

States. The U.S. quickly made it known that it did not support the actions of its allies, and public opinion began to swing in Egypt's favour. The move was largely seen as Britain and France, both former colonial powers, trying to maintain their colonial hold on the Middle East.

The United States wasn't the only country that didn't support the British. Canada also opposed its Commonwealth partner's actions. Pearson approached the United Nations with a proposal: create an international force through the United Nations to keep peace in the area. It was the birth of what would become a signature feature of the United Nations for decades afterwards, peacekeeping.

Meanwhile, Norman was hard at work in Egypt, trying to convince Nasser to agree to Pearson's proposal. Nasser, however, was skeptical. Even after six months of negotiations, on March 12, 1957, Nasser informed Norman that he would not agree to allow any Canadian soldiers to be on the proposed peacekeeping force. Back home, Pearson was facing criticism for not supporting the British. So he needed Canadian troops on the UN peacekeeping force in order to blunt some of that criticism.

But the sharks were still circling Norman. That same day, March 12, his name was again raised at the SISS. Those on the committee were unhappy to learn that Norman had been named ambassador to Egypt, especially when it was embroiled in the thick of an international controversy. Those on the committee were worried that Communists would take over Egypt and were determined to stop it.

Norman was able to schedule another meeting with Nasser, and after three hours, convinced the Egyptian president to accept Canadian troops as part of the peacekeeping force. Yet in the midst of what should have been Norman's greatest professional accomplishment, his enemies in the U.S. were determined to bring him down. Two days later, the senate committee attacked him again. They were also gunning for Pearson. The State Department was told of a former Soviet spy who was prepared to name Lester Pearson as a spy. Some in the U.S. wanted to release that information, but the higher-ups refused because Pearson was widely respected. The State Department, however, did allow Norman's detractors to continue to pursue him.

One week later, Norman learned in a letter from External Affairs that, despite its protests, the U.S. was going to continue its investigation of him. The committee even summoned his old friend, Shigeto Tsuru, to testify about his associations with Norman. It was a difficult time for Norman. He went to see his doctor in Egypt, who had prescribed sedatives for him, and he remarked that he was worried that his friends, including Pearson, were getting dragged into the situation. He grew increasingly depressed, spending much of his time in his office with the door closed, often laying on the couch and staring at the ceiling.

On April 3, Norman attended a special screening of a Japanese film at a nearby theatre. The following day, at approximately 8:30 AM, Norman travelled to the Wadi el Nil Building, where the Swedish Ambassador, a friend, kept his residence. Norman carried three notes, one for the Swedish Ambassador, apologizing for the use of his building but stating it was the only one he could think of where there was little risk of landing on a passerby. The other two notes were for his wife and his brother. One stated the following:

> *I am overwhelmed by consciousness of sin. May God in his infinite mercy forgive me if he will. Time and the record will show to any who is impartial and not want to make every unsolved case stick to my name that I am innocent on the central issue. I have never conspired or committed an act against the security of our state. Never have I violated my oath of secrecy. But how the issues will be obscured and twisted. But I am too tired of it all. The forces against me are too formidable, even for an innocent man and it is better to go now than to live indefinitely pelted with mud. The department will be greatly distressed at the possible implications of this, but I trust in an exhaustive and fair-minded study, which will uphold my innocence. Too many words. And I am too tired. Illusion has been my besetting weakness. Naïveté my chief flaw. I thought innocence against any act of security was enough. How naïve. My loved ones will regret this act, but I believe they will understand the reasons for it. In utter humility I beg their forgiveness.*

The press back in Canada were not quiet about who they believed responsible for Norman's death. The headline of the *Toronto Daily Star* contained a quote from MP Alistair Stewart, who stated that Norman was "murdered by slander, just as surely as if someone had stuck a knife in his back." Below the headline, possibly as a jab at whom they believed to be responsible, the paper ran a picture of Robert Morris, the counsel of the SISS, who had been so doggedly pursuing Norman over the years.

The following was written six months after Norman's death:

> *If Herbert Norman who so loved the good in men and had such faith in the power of reason to persuade men has ended his short life in the midst of fanaticism and prejudice and intolerance, what should we do, we who remain behind?*

In the days that followed, various newspapers published different versions of what it believed were Norman's actual suicide notes. But External Affairs refused to comment or release the actual notes in their possession, citing privacy for Norman's widow Irene. And as time passed, besides public anger towards the U.S., some began to wonder exactly why Norman had killed himself. It seemed unfathomable to anyone that an innocent person would so violently end his own life. It may have seemed more the act of a guilty person, someone with something to hide. That speculation was compounded by the fact that some of the media had publicly reported that one of Norman's suicide notes contained a line that seemed to indicate that he was taking the true reason for his suicide with him to the grave.

For decades afterwards, the question of Norman's guilt or innocence was left officially unanswered. At least one book was published that purported to detail Norman's Communist connections. In 1990, Joe Clark, then the Minister of External

Affairs, asked Peyton Lyon to conduct his own investigation into Norman's history.

Lyon's report, presented to Clark in 1991, found that Norman was neither a spy nor an agent of influence for any country. Lyon concluded that Norman had been a Communist while studying at Cambridge, and had still been one, but less so, afterwards when he studied at Harvard. He had cut his party associations but kept up friendships with known Marxists. He was never a member of the Communist Party in Canada, Britain or the United States, and while he did not lie about being a member of the party, he had "understated" the degree of his commitment and the knowledge of his activities. Lyon concluded that Norman had killed himself for the reasons Norman mentioned in his suicide notes, and determined that there had been no cover-up at any time indicating that Norman had been a spy or an agent of influence. Lyon concluded:

> *Herbert Norman was loyal to the people of Japan, the land of his childhood. He was loyal to humanity and to the pursuit of historical truth. He was loyal to himself; he never denounced the idealistic youth who misguidedly saw in Communism and the Soviet Union the only hope for civilized man. He was above all, loyal to his friends and to his country.*

Ultimately no one knows why Norman, who had accomplished so much and who knew he had friends back in Canada, namely Lester B. Pearson, who would fight for him, would choose suicide over fighting to clear his name. While some mystery remains, it seems that Norman's only crime was to think that communism might actually work. Of course, at the time of his death, many believed that was one of the worst beliefs a person could have. History, however, has proven such people wrong.

The Beothuk

~

When the Norse reached Newfoundland, the First Nations people they likely encountered were the Beothuk. What happened to this community of First People is a mystery.

The Beothuk were described as tall people with dark eyes and dark hair. As the Europeans descended on Newfoundland and settled it, the Beothuk were driven away from the area. Some were sent to Europe as slaves or put on display. The Beothuk tried to avoid contact with the Europeans, but as Europeans increasingly exploited the land, it made it more difficult for the Beothuk people to live their lives in their traditional way. The Beothuk also had no immunity against the diseases that the Europeans brought to the area, which ultimately decimated their population.

The last full-blooded Beothuk was a woman named Shanawdithit. She was found by Europeans in 1823 with two other Beothuk people who were sick and starving. The other two died, but Shanawdithit survived. She lived another six years before she died of tuberculosis.

With her death, the Beothuk people were no more.

~

Chapter 7

Jerome

~

One Canadian mystery about which much has been written but so little has been actually verified is that of a man named Jerome. It is not known with any degree of certainty if his name actually was Jerome, but it is what the residents of Digby Neck, Nova Scotia, christened him and, with little in the way of new information ever being found, the name has stuck.

Investigating the case of the man named Jerome brings to the forefront all manner of stories. What remains is that while people can say a great deal about Jerome, little of it is grounded in any kind of fact. Everything about the story of Jerome, from where he was found to what he was wearing to how he conducted himself and even when he died, has myriad details that change depending on the storyteller.

This is what is known as fact. One day, in the mid-to-late 1800s, a man was found on the shore of Sandy Cove, Nova Scotia. The man was found beside a large rock. The intriguing part of the find was that the man had no legs, and further inspection found that his legs had likely been amputated. The man also did not speak; he did not answer the questions that were asked of him. At one point, he made some noises that those who overheard him said sounded distinctly like the name Jerome, so the name stuck.

After he was found on the beach, Jerome lived in Digby Neck with various families until his care became too burdensome; it was believed he could do little for himself, and as a result, he required constant supervision. He was eventually taken to the nearby French community of Meteghan where he lived with a man named Jean Nicola. He lived there for seven years until Nicola moved back to Europe. Jerome was then moved to the home of Dedier and Zabeth (Elisabeth) Comeau in St. Alphonse, who charged people to come and see Jerome. The Nova Scotia government provided an allowance to compensate Jerome's caretakers for the costs associated with caring for him. Jerome stayed with the Comeaus until he died, sometime in the early 20th century.

That one paragraph pretty much sums up the total volume of fact in the case of Jerome. However, a great detail more remains to be shared, but so much of it, because it was passed down in the oral tradition cannot be substantiated. What follows is an attempt to impart as much detail as there is available in the public record. As to what is actually the truth, as is so often the case in matters such as these, is probably somewhere in the midst of all the details of all the stories told.

The date most often given when it comes to the case of Jerome of Sandy Cove, Nova Scotia, is 1863, although the years 1854 and 1861 have also been cited as the year that he was found. He is most commonly described as being found in early September. How he was found and who found him are issues that have never been definitively settled. A great deal of speculation surrounds what transpired in the days immediately preceding Jerome's discovery. In some accounts, nothing noteworthy occurred, and one day Jerome was suddenly just there. But most accounts include the story of a ship, visible from shore, sailing unusually just off Sandy Cove in the day or two before Jerome was found. The ship is described in some accounts as a warship of some kind, such as a European man-of-war. Other accounts describe two ships that appeared to be schooners anchored in Sandy Cove. Regardless of whether it was one ship or two, the ship(s) involved were observed to be behaving in a peculiar way in the days before Jerome was found. They were alternating sailing back and forth in the cove with resting at anchor. When the residents of Digby Neck awoke the morning Jerome was found, whatever ship or ships had been there had vanished.

How Jerome was found typically follows two narratives. In one case, an eight-year-old boy named George Colin "Collie" Albright, who just happened to be down on the beach, found Jerome. (It was said that once he grew older, George Albright became something of a hermit who would scavenge the beach for useful items and hex passing ships). Another account credits Jerome's discovery to Martin Albright, whose cottage offered a first-hand glimpse of whatever ship or ships had been acting so strangely in the cove. The day the ship(s) disappeared, Albright happened to look out his window and see what he thought was a group of otters frolicking by the large boulder on the beach. When he looked again later, he realized what he saw was not a group of otters but appeared to be a man on the beach. Other accounts have Martin walking along the beach when he spotted Jerome.

The consensus view is that Jerome, when he was found, was in a tough spot. He had no legs, only stumps where legs had once been. He could scarcely move himself, and the place where he was left was typically covered at high tide, which would likely have resulted in his drowning. He was cold and shivering and on the brink of hypothermia. But beyond these few facts, there is little agreement about exactly what happened and what the person who found Jerome actually found down on the shoreline.

In some accounts, they found Jerome trying to crawl back out to sea in an effort to drown himself. In most accounts, however, he was found propped against a large boulder on the beach. He was found with a cask of water and either a "tin of biscuits" or a loaf of coarse, black bread. Some accounts state that he was also found with a bundle of clothes in his possession. While there is no agreement on what he was wearing when found, it is agreed that whatever clothes he was wearing were of excellent quality. In some accounts, Jerome was wearing only some kind of undergarments that were soaked through. In other accounts, he was wearing something that appeared to be a naval uniform of deep navy blue. And in some of those accounts, the uniform appeared to have had its buttons, decorations, awards and other identifying marks removed. An inspection of his stumps revealed that the legs had been amputated, and it is pretty much agreed that the amputation had been done with some degree of skill, meaning it had likely been performed by a surgeon. The condition of the stumps and apparent timeframe of the surgery, however, are in dispute. By some accounts, the amputation had been done quite recently, the stumps not yet completely healed, covered in bandages and still bleeding. In other accounts the amputation appeared to have taken place in distant past, as the stumps were completely healed and not bandaged.

Every account agrees that Jerome didn't communicate with anyone. Where there seems to be no agreement is whether or not Jerome chose not to communicate or whether he was completely incapable of speaking. Whichever Albright found him either sent for help or managed to wave down some passersby, who took Jerome to the Albright home to convalesce and recover from the cold and exposure he had experienced. When they tried to talk to him, however, he did not reply. As his condition improved, many people passed through the Albright household, trying to elicit some kind of response from Jerome that might shed some light on who he was and where he came from. People who spoke French, Latin, Italian and Spanish came by and tried to talk to him, but Jerome gave no indication that he could, or wanted to, engage with them. What he often did was growl at people he did not want near him, and it was often described as sounding much like a dog's growl.

Some accounts that have been passed down through the years maintain that Jerome actually did speak a total of three words that were heard by more than one person. When he was asked for his name, he either clearly spoke or made sounds that sounded like the name Jerome. Regardless of whether or not he intended to say that specific word, it was the name he went by for the rest of his life. Other accounts state that when asked where he came from, he said something that sounded like "Trieste," which is the name of a city in northeast Italy. He was also believed to have said the word "*Colombo*," which was interpreted two ways by the locals. Some came to believe it was his last name while others came to believe that "*Colombo*" may have been the name of a ship on which he had served or on which he had come to Sandy Cove. Independent of his apparently having uttered the word Trieste, many in Digby Neck came to the conclusion that, based on his appearance, his ethnicity was Mediterranean in origin, possibly Italian.

While the people of Digby Neck tried to help Jerome, it quickly became clear that doing so was beyond the means of many residents there. He was passed from home to home, but few were able to look after Jerome for long. Digby Neck was also a Baptist community and, given that they had decided he was Mediterranean in origin, the people there presumed that he was also likely Catholic. Consequently, in what has been dated February 1864, the local Overseers of the Poor reasoned it was better to move Jerome to the nearby Francophone community of Meteghan. It was also around this time that the Government of Nova Scotia, having heard Jerome's story and of the hardship he was creating for those trying to care for him, approved a stipend of $2.00 per week ($104.00 per year) to offset some of the costs borne by anyone who took him in.

In Meteghan, Jerome was sent to stay with Jean Nicola. Although he was Corsican in origin and widely believed to be a deserter, Nicola was nicknamed "the Russian." Sending Jerome to stay with Nicola was a deliberate action. Nicola spoke many languages, and the hope was that if he tried speaking these various languages to Jerome, the man might eventually respond to one of them. But according to most accounts, Jerome never responded to anyone. Some suggested that he appeared to become more engaged or alert whenever he heard languages such as Italian or French being spoken, but these accounts are not consistent.

There is also a historical problem when it comes to the prevailing belief that Jerome was of Italian stock or descent or even that he spoke Italian. At the time that Jerome was found, Italy was not yet a unified country. It had been declared as a nation-state, but the final date of Italian unification is generally believed to be 1870, seven years after Jerome first appeared on the beach at Digby Neck. As a result of the somewhat fractured nature of Italy's unification, there was also no real thing as a common Italian language. Many regions spoke dialects that scarcely resembled what is known today as Italian. So to suggest that Jerome appeared Italian or seemed to respond when someone spoke Italian is somewhat inaccurate.

The ongoing issue of Jerome's lack of ability to communicate was also a problem. The stories of Jerome are split as to whether or not he did not speak because he was unable or because he simply chose not to. The belief that he was somehow mentally challenged came from the fact he did not speak with anyone, that he growled at people and made guttural sounds, and in some accounts, that he ate with his hands. But there are those who simply maintained that Jerome could comprehend everyone just fine and that for reasons known only to him, he chose not to speak to any of the adults who spent time with him. Some individuals noted that he could respond to basic commands such as, "Get up."

There was also division over what Jerome looked like. Some concluded that he appeared to be about 19 years old when he was found. Some described him as having flaxen hair and blue eyes, while others said his hair was lighter and his eyes were different colours as well. One belief that transcends all accounts of Jerome's appearance is that an inspection of his hands showed them to be soft and smooth, which the people of Digby Neck took to mean that he was not accustomed to manual labour. Some took this idea even further, stating that the condition of his hands, coupled (in some accounts) with the description of the high quality clothes he was found in, meant that Jerome was some sort of nobleman, which, as we shall see later, fed wild speculation about exactly who Jerome was and where he came from.

Jerome lived with Jean Nicola in Meteghan for seven years along with Jean' wife Julitte and his stepdaughter Madeleine.

But Julitte died, and as a result of her death, Nicola decided to return to Europe. And so Jerome was sent to St. Alphonse, which was then known as Cheticamp or Petit-Cheticamp, to live with Dedier and Zabeth Comeau, the four children they already had and the nine more they would eventually have.

At the Comeau household, Jerome was treated as something of a freak. The Comeaus charged people admission to come into their home and view Jerome. Letters and interviews from individuals endure from that time saying that people passing through the community, having heard of Jerome, would visit the Comeau home, typically on Sunday afternoons after mass. The Comeaus often kept him tethered with a chain affixed to one of his arms. In addition, the Comeau residence served as the community's coach stop, meaning individuals just passing through could stop in and pay to see Jerome. It was frequently recorded that Jerome didn't seem to mind being treated this way, or it was possible that he could not really comprehend what was happening. The Comeaus lived quite well as a result of housing Jerome, both on what they charged strangers to gawk at him and on the $2.00 per week stipend from the Nova Scotia government. On at least one occasion, Dedier took Jerome on the road, transporting him to Yarmouth and putting him on display at McLaughlin's Hall for people to come and ogle him.

Most accounts state that Jerome lived a low-key or "idle" life. He spent the winters holed up inside the Comeau's home, beside the wood stove, trying to stay warm. In the spring and summer, he would sit outside and bask in the sun or pull himself along on his stumps using his hands. At one point someone gave him a pair of leather caps that fit over the stumps of his legs; these offered him some protection as he pulled himself around.

While most seem to agree that Jerome couldn't or didn't want to speak to any adults, there are multiple accounts of his spending time with and, some say, even communicating with children. Most of these accounts were typically described as taking place whenever no adults were present. One individual recorded in an interview that when they spoke to him, Jerome made some mention of "chains." When they children asked him what happened to his legs, he responded with something to the effect of "sawed off on table."

In 1902, the Comeaus built a new, larger home in the community, and Jerome moved there with the family. Yet shortly after the house was finished, Dedier passed away. Jerome stayed with Zabeth and the family for what was believed to be another 10 years until he also passed away. The most common date of death given for Jerome is April 15, 1912, the same day that the RMS *Titanic* sank. The death certificate for Jerome lists the cause of death as bronchitis, and there is a note that Jerome had been sick in the three weeks preceding his death, and that he was baptized shortly after he became ill. The date of his burial is listed as April 18. He was interred at the cemetery in the Roman Catholic parish of Meteghan. The age listed on the death certificate is 85, which conflicts with the prevailing view that Jerome was 19 or 20 when he was found. If he was 85 when he died, then Jerome would have been about 36 years old when he was found, which is a far cry from 19 or 20. If he was

19 or 20 when he was found, then he would have been in his late 60s when he died.

While a record exists of where Jerome was buried, there seems to be some dispute about whether or not his actual resting place in the cemetery is known. Some accounts state that his grave is clearly marked, while others say that no one really knows where his body is buried. In 2000, a stone marker was placed in the Meteghan parish cemetery in Jerome's honour. The stone includes a plaque and copy of the only known picture of him.

And now to the biggest question that has trickled down through history over the last 150-plus years since Jerome was first found. Who was he, and where did he come from?

There are myriad theories that claim to answer these basic questions, yet few contain enough solid evidence to conclusively link Jerome to any of the wild stories that have been cooked up about his origins. Most theories contain a significant amount of unsupported conjecture. And while some oral histories that have been passed down might seem plausible, few contain any rock-solid evidence or documentation.

As stated earlier, it was noted by many that Jerome's hands did not show any signs that he was a labourer, which, when viewed alongside the supposed fine quality of the clothes he was found in, led many to believe that Jerome was some sort of nobleman. Adherents to this theory managed to cook up some of the most compelling and outlandish explanations for Jerome's appearance. They believed that, if Jerome was some kind of nobleman, that he had been left in Nova Scotia as a result of a squabble over an inheritance. That is, some jealous family members either had his legs amputated and had him shipped off or that his legs had already been amputated, and he was placed on a boat and taken away. Others said his legs were amputated, and he was punished because, as a nobleman, he was believed to have participated in some sort of nefarious plot. The same theory also holds that Jerome was silent by choice, as he did not want to say anything that might lead to the discovery of his origins.

A variation on the theory of Jerome being a nobleman is said to include some sort of documentation from Jerome himself. The story goes that, many years after Jerome died, a descendant of Dedier Comeau was renovating the family home. He was pulling boards off the walls when he noticed one plank that was out of alignment with the rest, as if it had been removed and then put back in place. When the he pulled the board away, a sheaf of yellowed papers came flying out onto the floor. The writing on the papers was in a language that no one locally recognized. The papers eventually found their way into the hands of a foreign language expert who translated the documents into French, although from what language originally no one knows.

The writer identifies himself as Jerome, and goes on to explain that he was a nephew of Emperor Franz Joseph I, Emperor of Austro-Hungarian Empire and the last Hapsburg ruler of that country. Jerome goes on to write that one day, he witnessed an assassination attempt on his uncle's life in which the emperor was nearly killed. In order to save his own life,

Jerome fled the empire, drawing on his years at naval college to serve aboard a man-of-war. After a year of service, Jerome returned to Austria-Hungary. Shortly after he returned, he was captured by unknown men who wanted to murder him to ensure he'd never be able to say who had tried to assassinate his uncle. Jerome pleaded for his life, and his captors relented, swearing him to secrecy. To ensure his secrecy, they took him to a hospital. He was told they were going to ensure that he could never return to implicate anyone. At the hospital, his legs were amputated. He was placed aboard the man-of-war named *Colombo* and left on the shores of Boston, Massachusetts. A family there took him in, but when they became unable to care for him, he was placed aboard another European man-of-war and taken to Sandy Cove.

There was an attempt to assassinate Emperor Joseph recorded as taking place on February 18, 1853, when a Hungarian nationalist named János Libényi tried to stab the emperor in the neck from behind. The military uniform the emperor wore had a sturdy, high neck that deflected most of the knife blow. While he was left bloodied from the attack, the emperor survived. Libényi was subdued on the spot by an Irish nobleman who had been walking with the emperor and a butcher who happened to be nearby. Libényi was put on trial and executed for attempted regicide eight days later. Given that it appears the emperor's would-be assassin was subdued on the spot then captured and executed, it seems highly unlikely that Jerome's account is accurate.

Emperor Joseph did have nephews because he had three brothers, and his personal life was somewhat tragic. One of his brothers, Maximilian, the short-lived Emperor of Mexico, was executed in 1867; Maximilian's son Crown Prince Rudolf killed himself in 1889; and his wife was assassinated in 1898. Joseph also had one famous nephew, a young archduke named Franz Ferdinand, who went on to play a significant role in one of modern history's most ferocious conflicts, World War I. Given that any nephew would have been a relatively high-profile member of the royal family, it is extremely unlikely that one member would have been able to vanish without a trace and no mention of it in the historical record.

The theory of Jerome as royalty, however, does have some elements that appear in other stories. One story mentions the Gidney family that put their ship into port in Maine in 1879. While there, two men approached them. They were interested in speaking to anyone from Nova Scotia. The men asked questions about a legless castaway. One of the men explained that 16 years earlier he had been paid to take a legless man to Nova Scotia. The story goes on that Jerome had been a castaway on an Italian ship sailing for New Brunswick. When he arrived in New Brunswick, he worked odd jobs around St. John, including a stint in a lumber camp. While working in the lumber camp, he became lost in the nearby woods. He managed to stumble into an old sawmill where he was found near death. He was taken to Gagetown where his legs were amputated because they were frozen and therefore useless. The community eventually decided it didn't want the burden of caring for him, so they hired a man to take him across the bay to Nova Scotia.

There are close parallels between this latter story and another that many believe is the most likely explanation for Jerome's origins. The story is that of a man named Gamby, who, depending on which account you hear, either fell through ice into a lake or was found in dire straits on a logging trail in 1859. He was given a place to stay in Chipman Parish, and his legs, which eventually developed gangrene because they had been frozen, were amputated. He was given the name Gamby because, as the story goes, when he awoke, he cried out "*gambe*," which is Italian for "legs." Gamby eventually became too much of a burden, so the community paid a ship's captain to take him away. That captain simply dumped him on the other side of the Bay of Fundy. While this theory is plausible, it has been criticized as speculative and pure fiction. It also doesn't offer a reason for Jerome/Gamby's refusal or inability to communicate.

A rash of theories about Jerome's origins focus on the fact that he came from a ship. Adherents to these theories state that Jerome may have been a sailor of some sort, either a naval officer or a pirate. In either account, Jerome's legs were amputated on the ship. In some variations of the naval or pirate story, Jerome's legs were amputated as punishment for mutiny. In other variations, they were amputated as a result of an accident on board. However none of these stories account for the fact that it would be unlikely that a pirate ship would carry a skilled surgeon. Almost all accounts state that the amputation was performed by a person with some skill. The navy variation doesn't wash either because it seems highly unlikely that a navy captain would abandon a member of his crew that he went to the trouble of saving when he ordered the ship's surgeon to amputate the man's legs. In neither the pirate nor the navy version does it make sense that a sailor would be punished in such a way for mutiny. The most frequent punishment for mutiny in the 1800s was death. It also seems unlikely that neither pirate nor ship's captain would go to the trouble of skilfully removing a man's legs then transporting him to shore and abandoning him as a kind of punishment. However, there are anecdotal reports that Jerome, despite being generally mild-mannered, would fly into a rage that lasted for days whenever he heard the words "pirate" or "traitor."

The remaining theories have fewer details but they exist nonetheless. It's been suggested that Jerome was a murderer fleeing from justice. None of these theories explain how a legless man would a) have committed murder, or b) have escaped to the shores of Nova Scotia. Some have offered that he was a spy or army deserter, but the details on either of these theories are sparse. Others simply believe he knew some terrible secret, and he never spoke out of fear. Others said he was American or Irish but offered little more about how he had come to lose his legs or to be left stranded in Nova Scotia.

Many other anecdotes have been reported from Jerome's life that, if they are to be believed, would offer clues as to Jerome's origins. In one instance, when Jerome was living with the Comeaus, two women appeared one day at the home and asked to speak to Jerome in private. The women went into a room with Jerome and were overheard speaking to Jerome. Apparently those attempting to eavesdrop also heard a male voice in the conversation, and they believed it to be Jerome's voice since no other male was in the room. When the two women left, they were overheard to say something to the effect of, "He's well here. Let's just leave him."

There is another story about women and Jerome. One day, either the Comeaus were in New York or one of Dedier's sons, Charles, was working in New York, when either one or two women visited him. The woman/women, who were from Alabama, had heard about Jerome and wondered if he might be her/their long-lost brother. In one variation, the women had the last name Mahoney and said that their brother had run away three times before he turned 11, and then he finally ran away for good the fourth time. Their father spent the rest of his life looking for the boy. The woman/women gave the Comeaus/Charles a letter, which they took to Jerome. Jerome took the envelope, examined it and tore it into pieces without reading it. Another variation of the story states that Jerome one day received a letter, which he threw into the fire without reading.

The only thing that can be said for certain when it comes to Jerome's story is that no one really knows who he was or where he came from. Given that more than 150 years have passed and no one has been able to unearth any real evidence about who he might have been, it seems highly unlikely that an answer will ever be forthcoming.

Who Discovered the East Coast
of Canada First?

~

When I was in junior high, my fellow pupils and I first learned of the history of Canada (in French class, no less), and our teacher of the time framed the discovery of Canada by Europeans as almost a kind of contest. First came John Cabot just before the beginning of the 16th century. But he didn't do much with his finding on behalf of the Portuguese. But then came Jacques Cartier in 1534, whose discovery of Canada was thought to be more significant because it led to the first colonies on the island of what is now Montréal.

But it turns out that Cabot and Cartier were not the first Europeans to land in what is now Canada. In fact, the Norse, were the first Europeans to set foot on Canadian land a half a century before even Christopher Columbus discovered America in 1492. First came Bjarni Herjólfosson, who was allegedly blown off course while travelling between Iceland and Greenland; he landed in the summer of either 985 or 986. Approximately 15 years later, Leif Ericson landed at three different places in Canada, described in Norse history as Helluland, Markland and Vinland. Helluland is believed to have been Baffin Island, Markland was possibly Labrador and Vinland was likely Newfoundland. The Norse made an attempt at colonization—one settlement was found in Newfoundland—but it is believed that the weather and problems with the First Nations of the time led the Norse to abandon their colonies.

~

Chapter 8

William Robinson

~

Salt Spring Island has always been a refuge of sorts. Tucked away in the Strait of Georgia, just off the coast of Vancouver Island, the small chunk of land in the strait is a welcoming place. The temperature seldom dips below zero degrees Celsius and while there might a be a lot of rain, there is also a great deal of beauty, an abundance of fresh seafood, and in the late 1800s, a small population. It's a small island, measuring only 182.7 square kilometres in area, but that small island once stood as a beacon of hope to African Americans looking to escape racism and oppression in the United States. Various Salishan peoples settled there before the pioneers came, around 1859, when it was called Admiral Island. Those people who settled it were mostly farmers who came west searching for arid land for their crops.

Other people came to the island as well looking to escape. In the years leading up to the American Civil War, racism in the United States was endemic and slavery was still legal. Many African Americans made their way to Canada on the Underground Railroad in the hopes of finding freedom. Salt Spring Island became a place for African Americans to resettle.

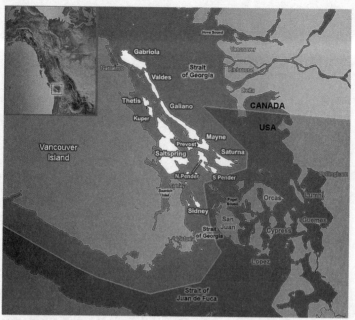

The Southern Gulf Islands, including Salt Spring Island. It was the first Gulf Island to be settled and the first farming in the Colony of Vancouver Island.

~

Specifically, several African Americans from California came to the island around the time the first pioneers did. They were trying to escape racist laws that had been passed in that state. They found, not just on Salt Spring Island, but also on some parts of Vancouver Island, places where they could build a life and work free of the oppressive racism. But even though they were free, these new settlers were not necessarily safe. In the 1860s, terrible events occurred on Salt Spring Island.

William Robinson was one such African American who had escaped the United States, coming to the island by himself in the mid 1860s, looking to be left alone. At the time, Salt Spring Island and British Columbia were colonies of Great Britain. The island was sparsely populated, with only about 25 pioneer families calling it home. Aboriginal people also lived close by, and the people of Salt Spring Island often found themselves in conflict with them. The residents fired off letters to their British overseers, demanding more funding for things like roads and schools, saying that other communities nearby had received more funding than they had. They would howl about how vulnerable they were and beg for their government in Britain to do more to protect them. Every so often, the British would send a gunboat into the region. The vessel would dock at the harbour, and the sailors on board would make a show of beating the bushes, even firing off a few rounds. Then they would leave.

It is unlikely that many of the reports of savagery and open confrontation with the Aboriginal people of the island were true, but it does paint a tense picture of life on Salt Spring Island. And in the middle of that tension lived a small community of African Americans, one of whom was William Robinson. He had a small patch of land, land that was later believed to be quite valuable, and he grew some crops on that land. He went to church on Sundays and, for the most part, kept to himself. He helped others when they needed it and was, for the most part, seen as a member of the larger community. He was described as "inoffensive" and "harmless." He lived by himself in a log house that was described as "rather lonely."

One day, in March 1868, a member of the community went by Robinson's house with what was described as some "goods" for Robinson. He knocked on the door, but no one came. He peered through a gap in the logs of the home and saw a man's boots lying on the floor. The man grabbed a nearby stick and pushed it through the gap, touching the boots, and "...perceiving no motion, [he] gave the alarm."

The constable on the island, one Henry Sampson, came after he was fetched, which appears to have been on a Monday.

Dubbed "the Father of British Columbia" James Douglas was the governor of the Colony of Vancouver Island, which included Salt Spring Island. His mother was of mixed black and white ancestry. He replied in the affirmative to a request from black settlers to move to the colony.

The constable came by, but found the door locked. He pried free a log near the door and was able to use that to get inside. Inside, he found the body of William Robinson. The description given at the time was that Robinson was found on the floor of his cabin, lying on his back. In between his knees was a box that the constable surmised Robinson had been sitting on. Clutched in his hand was a knife, "which he was in the act of conveying food to his mouth and had so lain to all appearances probably a week."

Sampson examined the body and found that Robinson had been shot. It appeared the ball from whatever firearm had been used had passed through Robinson's back and exited his chest. There were burn marks from the gunpowder on his clothes, indicating that the gun had likely been fired at close range. For reasons that were never explained, those clothes were buried with Robinson's body instead of being preserved as evidence. A closer look actually turned up two holes in Robinson's body, with the second hole apparently passing from the chest to the back.

"The assassin was probably sitting at the man's own hearth," stated a report on Robinson's death published in *The British Colonist*.

Closer examination of the small cabin revealed that some items were believed to be missing, including a double-barrel shotgun, some clothes and "the man's account books." There were later mentions of a "chest" of some sort belonging to Robinson that might also have been missing. Further examination of the room turned up one of the balls from the firearm.

"A feeling of great insecurity prevails among the settlers, who frequently have valuable cattle shot by unknown hands. Many of the colored settlers have their wives and families there, whom they hardly dare leave for a day alone," said the *Colonist* story.

What was more distressing than the fact Robinson had been apparently murdered in his own home at very close range was the fact that he was not the first African American on the island to have been murdered. On August 1, 1867, the body of a black man was found buried and partially decomposed in an old stonecutter's house at the quarry at north end of the island. The cabin in which the remains were found had been partially burnt. While the identity of the dead man was never truly established, there were reports that two black men had been living in the cabin during the previous winter. An examination of the remains seemed to indicate that the person had been murdered, and it also appeared that the victim was African American. People thought the clothes on the body might have matched the clothes that one of the black men, known as Bill, had been wearing. Some believed that, if the person was in fact one of the two black men seen there the previous winter, it was entirely likely he had been killed by his friend.

"They had a spade and an axe with them, they frequently quarrel'd between themselves," one Edward Williams told the authorities.

James Ogilvy, a ferry operator, found the body. He said he had been at the quarry to pick up a load of stone to take to New Westminster. When he went inside the house, he noticed the floor inside had given away a bit. When he dug down into the floor, he found the body. The local constables tried to follow up a few leads. The most promising leads were reports of a man who had been seen in the area around the time that the building had been on fire. He carried a gun and was accompanied by a dog. And most people knew exactly who that man was. He was Thomas Griffiths, a man who lived on the island and was known to own a lot of cattle. When interviewed later by the authorities about what he had been doing near the cabin with a gun and dog around the time of the fire, Griffiths explained that he had been looking for some of his cows. In a strange twist, Griffiths was named the foreman of the jury at the inquest into the man's death. Perhaps unsurprisingly, the jury ruled that the man had in fact died, but there was no evidence to prove how he had died.

Back at the William Robinson crime scene, Constable Sampson sent for the coroner, but the coroner didn't arrive until the following day. An inquest was held. Some records indicate that two men were arrested, and some testimony by Constable Sampson seems to indicate that he suspected Manuel Duwet (or Duett) and Clarke Whims. But Sampson later clarified that Whims was never a suspect, and Sampson had only interviewed him to see if he knew anything. It was apparently Clarke's brother William that gave evidence to lead to the most likely suspect, and of course, that person turned out to be Aboriginal.

One member of the community, John Norton, gave a sworn statement that he'd had an encounter with a group of "strange Indians" fishing near his house. A week after he saw them, one of these men went to Norton and told him that he knew who had killed Robinson. He identified the killer as a "Chemainus Indian named Tom that shot him," and that "another Indian of Plumbers Pass" had been with this Tom on the night that it happened. He also told Norton that the gun that had been taken from Robinson's house was in a box in Tom's home.

Based on this evidence, the constable, accompanied by Norton, arrested Tom. While they were arresting him, they found an auger that they believed had come from Robinson's house, and when they loaded Tom into the canoe, they put the auger in the canoe as well. Unfortunately, something happened to the auger.

"We brought the auger away and put it into the Canoe. It was dark when we got to Salt Spring Island and then we could not find it. It must have been thrown overboard," Norton also wrote in his statement.

Sampson also took the sworn testimony of one Sue Tas, also known as Dick, described as the "Indian of Plumber's Pass" who had been described to Norton. According to Dick, he had been with Tom, travelling in a canoe. He said that when they stopped the canoe, Tom had gone up to the Robinson house, while Dick had at first stayed with the canoe. Then Dick also went up to the house to warm himself at the fire.

When Dick arrived at the house, he found Robinson cooking food. He said Tom told him that if he shot Robinson, that Dick was to go in and search the house for valuables.

Dick wanted no part of the plan, so he left and returned to the canoe. Shortly after he left, he heard a gunshot, followed by Tom calling him.

"I went to the door and looked in and saw the black man lying on the floor, I saw blood running out of his nose, and from his back. Tom told me to come in and get some things, I said no," Dick said.

Instead, Tom apparently helped himself to whatever he could find. That included an auger, a box and a cart, which were placed in the canoe. Tom then locked the door to Robinson's home and threw the key into the water. When they returned to their home at Chemainus, Dick said he saw Tom place the box from Robinson's home on a shelf in his house. He also said that he saw Tom take Robinson's gun into his own home.

Tom gave a completely different story in his own sworn statement, saying he had never been anywhere near the Robinson home.

"I don't know what the witness Dick wants to say, perhaps he wants to see me kill'd," Tom first said, before adding there was no way he could have been the one to kill Robinson.

"I have been sick two years. I went to New Westminster and got fire sick and could go about. Mr. Franklin new me to be a good Indian and made me a constable," Tom apparently said.

Tom was charged with Robinson's murder and bound over for trial, which was held in June 1869. Tom entered a plea of not guilty, and was represented at his trial by a Mr. Ring.

John Norton took the stand and offered more testimony than had originally been contained in his sworn statement. When he entered the cabin with Sampson, he said he noted that Robinson had been preparing mashed potatoes, salmon and bread for his dinner. The first wound they noticed had entered Robinson' body between the shoulder blades and exited the chest, while there was a second wound to Robinson's chest. Norton also talked about the night he went with Sampson to arrest Tom.

As stated in the transcript of Norton's testimony:

> I was present when the Prisoner was arrested. He was arrested in his own house. I saw an auger on the floor. I picked the auger up. It was like one Robinson had got for me. He had broken one of mine & given me one instead what this was like. I took it to the canoe with the Prisoner & took him to SS Island & when we got there it was night the auger was missed.

Norton also told the court that he had seen Tom in the area a month before and that he had seen him selling salmon to settlers, as well as hunting deer. This testimony was meant to refute Tom's assertion that he had been left too weak from being fire sick to have killed William Robinson.

A lot of testimony also came to light about an axe, yet in reviewing all of the sworn statements from the first few days after Robinson's body was found, there was no mention of an axe. But at trial, several witnesses were asked about an axe that the Crown now had in its possession. It turned out that this axe had been "found" in Tom's house on May 5, 1869, more than a year after Robinson was murdered and barely a month before the trial started. Tom had been in custody when his house was searched and the axe found. The constable had suddenly been told to look for an axe, which he said he found and recognized.

"I found the axe in the Prisoner's house laying down in a corner plain to see," Sampson later testified.

A great deal of testimony was recorded about whether or not the axe that was found was Robinson's, but most people who took the stand asserted that it was, saying they recognized the oak handle, the different chips and marks on it, as well as the slightly different set up, which was meant to account for the fact that Robinson had been left-handed. In rebuttal, the defence called to the stand a Thomas George Askew, a mill owner, who testified that he sold Tom an axe head, and that axe head from the axe in court looked a great deal like the one he had sold Tom. But he did not recognize the handle, and he would tell the court, "I do not swear that I sold the axe shown me to the Prisoner."

Dick was also called to the stand and told much the same story he had told when giving his sworn statement. He said that on the day they were together, Tom had been carrying his musket with him and that he had told Dick that he wanted to kill "the colored man." He testified that he saw Tom inside the cabin and that Robinson had returned to the table to eat his food. Dick then left, and when he heard a shot he went back. He said he saw Tom take a gun, an auger, a box, a coat, and now, an axe, when they left, and that Tom had taken all of these items back to his house. When shown the axe, Dick testified that it looked like the one that Tom had shown him in his home.

When asked by the defence why he didn't try to warn Robinson about Tom and what he was up to, Dick testified that he thought Tom would have killed him if he had done so.

The all-white jury retired at 4:55 PM to consider its verdict. They returned at 5:50 PM. Their verdict was predictable. Tom was found guilty and sentenced to death by hanging. He was transferred to Victoria, where he was to be hung at the gaol. His execution was scheduled for July 24, at 7:00 AM.

One record of the hanging records the following:

The condemned man made an effort to address his people, who pressed around the gallows, but his voice was choked and his sentences unintelligible. He was hanged shortly after 7 o'clock and seemed to suffer little or no pain. The lesson will prove a salutary one to the Indians.

Perhaps worth noting is the fact that, according to some records from the era, between 1861 and 1863, seven Aboriginals were hanged for their crimes. Editorials in some newspapers often stated that, in order to deal with the "threat" from the Aboriginal population, the authorities should just start arresting entire tribes until they gave up the names of those who were responsible for any crimes.

There are other records; however, that point to alternative theories about who may have killed William Robinson. The issue of how to properly dispose of Robinson's estate became quite heated at one point on the island. Robinson had not left a will, so the local justice of the peace, John Morely, was appointed by the court as executor of the estate. An accounting of all of Robinson's possessions read as follows:

- *Purse and apparel* *$23.24*

- *Effects in the house* .... *$8.37 ½*

- *Bacon* *$9.00*

- *Small quantity of Oates* *$7.00*

- *Cut Hay* *$12.00*

- *Hay and Straw* *$20.00*

- *5 Small pigs* *$8.00*

- *Improvements on land* *$100.00*

Total of .... *$187.82 ½*

These totals were later amended, without explanation, to the following:

- *1868 Purse and apparel* *$23.24*

- *Effects in the house* *$8.75*

- *Bacon:* *$15.00*

- *Oates* .... *$5.87 ½*

- *Hay* *$12.00*

- *Straw* *$30.00*

- *Five small pigs* *$8.00*

Total .... *$202.87 ½*

The total value of these possessions was offset by $89.66 ½ in expenses, which included messenger and stamp costs, the digging of Robinson's grave, as well as several other small expenses incurred as a result of executing Robinson's estate. It is not known why a second accounting of his effects showed greater value for some items than the first accounting.

The issue of Robinson's land also caused problems. Robinson's land was seen as being valuable because it was the only piece of land nearby where the mail steamer could land on that part of the island. Estimates written by angry members of the community said Robinson's land was likely valued at around $400 or $500, with the improvements on the land adding another $100 to $150 to that total, a fairly large sum in the 1860s. But for some reason, none of Robinson's land was ever put up for auction. It was later revealed that John Morley, the appointed executor of the estate, had simply purchased most of the farmland, and auctioned the remainder privately. Apparently, some of the land was sold to a Mr. Lester, but it's not known who that was. Morley claimed that the estate was not worth enough to actually cover the costs of paying to bring an auctioneer to the community to auction off the land and effects.

Morley got a surprise several years later when he received a claim from the United States. In 1872, Morley received a letter from someone representing Mrs. Mary Robinson, living in the United States. She claimed that she had been married to William Robinson, and that they had four children together: Rosetta, William, Charles and Harriet. Only Harriet was under the age of 18. Apparently Robinson had left them in the U.S. to come to Canada and had been just about to rejoin them when he was killed.

If Robinson hadn't been killed for his land, it may be that it was a story of revenge. A man named Thomas Crosby eventually told a story that many felt explained Robinson's murder. Apparently before the murder, some Natives in the area had been visited by some white men "in a sloop laden with grog." When one of the chiefs asked the men aboard the sloop for more grog, a fight broke out and the white men on board the sloop killed the Aboriginal chief and one other chief as well. The Aboriginals allegedly swore revenge on any white man they could find.

Shortly afterwards John Brown, a white man, was found killed at Cowichan. Then Robinson was killed. After Robinson's death, another white man named Hamilton was killed near Nanaimo, also on Vancouver Island. The story was never verified, and there seems to be an obvious flaw in the story, given that the Aboriginals allegedly swore vengeance upon white men, whereas Robinson was African American.

But what was most telling was the fact that, after Robinson was killed, another black man was found murdered as well. On December 13, 1868, about eight months after Robinson's death, a black man named Giles Curtis was found dead inside a home on a property belonging to the Stark family. He had apparently been shot and nearly decapitated with a knife found at the scene. Curtis and a man named Howard Estes had been tasked with looking after the property. Estes had been at church, and when he returned home, he found Curtis' body. The house was ransacked, and 10 shirts, two new axes and a sack of flour were taken, yet a purse with some money in it was left behind. When questioned, some people gave the name of a First Nations man named Jim as the possible perpetrator. Constable Sampson was called in to investigate, and he came to the conclusion that killer must be Aboriginal. He came to that conclusion after smelling a gun cover found in the home and stating that it smelled like salmon. He reasoned that, because local Aboriginals often ate salmon, they must have touched the gun cover and left the aroma of salmon on it. The same John Norton who had offered testimony in Robinson's murder stated that some Natives nearby had recently threatened him. Some huts at a nearby Aboriginal camp were searched but none of the stolen goods were found. The British Navy came in to assist with the investigation and rounded up several Aboriginal people, but no one was ever arrested.

Almost 10 years later, a man named Willy Selcatcher was accused of the murders. It was reported that Willy was arrested for "having shot someone named Richardson at Chemainus" according to testimony from Willy's brother's wife. In the end, the evidence wasn't enough for a jury, and Willy was acquitted of the charges. But the fact that another African American was killed only five months after the man who had apparently killed William Robinson was executed seems to lend credence to the theory that Tom, also known as Tshuanahusset, might not have been responsible for Robinson's murder. Remember too that Robinson was the second African American to be murdered on the island. No one had ever convicted or charged for the murder of the man whose remains were found in the stonecutter's cottage the year before Robinson was killed.

Another violent murder occurred after Tom's execution as well. On August 10, 1869, an Aboriginal named Charlie was found dead in a canoe. He was described as a hardworking, industrious man who worked for the settlers in the area. His wife told investigators that one day, he bought three bottles of whisky from a passing sloop. He drank one of the bottles himself, and then gave the rest to two other Natives who were there. When Charlie moved down the beach to sleep, his wife saw the two Aboriginals that had been drinking with him move down the beach to the same area. When she awoke, she found Charlie in a canoe dead, his throat cut, his head nearly cut off. No one was ever arrested and charged with Charlie's murder.

The evidence available today, while it doesn't point conclusively to any one person, raises more questions than it answers about just who might have been responsible for William Robinson's murder.

Klondike Gold Rush

~

The Klondike Gold Rush was a defining chapter in the history of western and northern Canada. But who started it all?

There are five individuals who are seen by different supporters as being responsible for first discovering gold in the Klondike. They are George Carmack, an American, and Canadians Skookum Jim, Kate Carmack, Dawson Charley and Robert Henderson. Skookum, Kate Carmack and Charley were all First Nations.

Henderson's claim is easiest to dismiss in a sense. It is known that he did not actually find gold first, but the contention is that he told George Carmack that Bonanza Creek would be a good place to start looking. Indeed it is Carmack's signature on an application for discovery claim on Bonanza Creek that has caused many to think that he should be credited with the gold's discovery.

Some accounts state that Skookum Jim had, in fact, found signs of gold in the area as early as two days prior to Henderson directing Carmack to the area. But it is difficult to distinguish among these three as to who may have found the gold first. Kate Carmack was married to George Carmack, and Skookum Jim was Kate's brother. The three were travelling with their nephew Dawson Charlie near Rabbit Creek when they spotted the glint of gold through the water. They staked their claim the following morning.

The Canadian government later acknowledged Henderson as being the person to officially discover gold in the Klondike, although his claim to fame may be more due to his Canadian citizenship than any real credit when it came to finding gold.

Chapter 9
Gerald Bull

~

It is probably reasonable to assume that the list of Canadians who have been assassinated by agents of a foreign government is quite small. That makes the tale of Gerald Bull and the circumstances of his death all the more intriguing. That he was deliberately murdered is beyond question. Most reports from the time of his death in March 1990 say he was killed when he was hit by five bullets, two to the head and three to the back. Exactly who fired those bullets and why they were ordered to do so is not known with any certainty. Ideas and theories are plentiful, some stronger than others, but nothing concrete and irrefutable exists. Given Bull's life and the activities in which he was engaged at the time of his death, it is more likely that he was the victim of a deliberate plot to kill him and not of a random crime. No, the life of Gerald Bull reads like something of a spy thriller; the story has even featured prominently in a book by Frederick Forsyth.

It became quite apparent when he was a young boy that Gerald Bull was going to grow up to make things. He was one of 10 children born to George and Gertrude Bull in North Bay, Ontario. Gerald was born March 9, 1928, but the family into which he was born soon changed drastically. His mother died after complications from giving birth to the family's last child. His father, a lawyer who had several loans called in when the stock market crashed to kick off the Great Depression, suffered what has been described as a nervous breakdown and started drinking heavily. The children were all sent to live with various relatives. Gerald went to live with Laura, one of his older sisters. Unfortunately, Laura died of cancer, and an aunt and uncle took him in. These people were relatively well off, and in 1938 they paid for him to attend the Regiopolis College, a school run by Jesuits, even though at the time he wasn't old enough to attend. He joined the school's model club and began designing and making his own airplanes out of balsa wood.

When he graduated from school in 1946, he entered Queen's University with a hope of entering officers' training school. His uncle was able to secure him a spot at the University of Toronto's medical school, but Bull declined because he preferred to apply for a spot at the university's new aeronautical engineering school. Even though he was only 16, Bull was granted admission, a result in no small part of the limited qualifying criteria required for the brand new program. He graduated in 1948 and was remembered more for his mediocrity than anything else. His intellect might have been average but his energy was tremendous. It was on the basis of this that, after working at a drafting job with A.V. Roe Canada, he was able to join the university's new Institute of Aerodynamics, securing one of only 12 positions. He was tasked with designing and building a supersonic wind tunnel that could generate significant speeds. The story goes that the institute wanted the wind tunnel done and ready to show off when it officially opened its doors. Bull and his fellow students worked until 3:30 AM to finish it, but they didn't bother testing it. When a military official pressed the button to start the wind tunnel, nothing happened. Someone else reached around and pushed the button harder, and it worked.

By 1950, Bull had finished his PhD, and when he defended his thesis in 1951, he was only 23, the youngest PhD in the institute's history. He was working at the Canadian Armament and Research Development Establishment or CARDE. CARDE was a joint Canadian and British group that was studying artillery, ballistics, supersonic flight, rockets and missile projects. As part of his work with CARDE, Bull was asked to build another wind tunnel, but the design he finally settled on was seen as too expensive. So Bull came up with a much cheaper and more innovative idea. Rather than placing models inside a wind tunnel, he proposed firing them out of a large gun, such as a military artillery piece. The models were enclosed inside an artillery round known as a sabot. When the gun was fired, the pieces of the sabot stripped away in flight, exposing the model. The model was fired through a series of cards placed 100 yards apart. The model was covered in a metallic coating that transferred to the cards as it passed through them, allowing Bull and other researchers to time the flight progress and motion of the model and measure its velocity.

In 1951, he met Noemi Gilbert when, after a fishing trip, he stopped by a local doctor's house to drop off some of the fish he had caught. Noemi was the doctor's daughter. Even though they were hardly ever able to spend time together because of Bull's schedule, they became engaged in February 1954 and married in July of the same year. They had two sons, Michael and Phillip.

Bull was often difficult to deal with. He was seen as temperamental, stubborn and "high-spirited." He had a near clinical loathing of bureaucracy and absolutely abhorred having to spend any amount of his time doing paperwork. But people were willing to put up with his truculence because of his ingenuity. In 1955, he successfully built a hypersonic wind tunnel for only $60,000 using scrap metal. As funding for CARDE decreased over time, Bull did what he could to move the money around to keep his projects going. He studied methods of detection using infrared and radar cross sections. He began working with a colleague to see if their gun-firing method of testing rocket and missile models could also be used to test aircraft in the design phase. He was even able to put some of his work to use in testing a new fighter, the CF-105 Avro Arrow. But Bull's attitude still caused headaches for his superiors. Shortly after the launch of *Sputnik 1* in 1957 by the Soviet Union, Bull leaked a totally fabricated story that Canada was close to unveiling a technology that would see a gun placed inside and fired from a United States Army missile. The furor over the story even reached Parliament Hill, and Prime Minister John Diefenbaker was forced to deny that any such plans existed.

Gerald Bull at the Space Research Institute, McGill University (Montréal) in 1964

Eventually, Bull's loathing of paperwork allegedly led to his departure from CARDE, when after a fight with a superior over completing paperwork, he tendered his resignation. But he wasn't out of work for long. McGill University soon hired him as a professor. He and Noemi bought a 2000-acre plot of land that straddled the border between Québec and Vermont and donated some of the land to the university for use as a new ballistics lab. What evolved from his work with the university was the High Altitude Research Project, or HARP. HARP had numerous goals. It was supposed to use large guns to shoot missile parts high into the air so their re-entry could be studied, an important consideration in the Cold War because the U.S. and Soviet Union were looking to increase the ranges of their nuclear-tipped missiles. Using a gun was substantially cheaper than actually firing missiles and studying them. But Bull also had an eye to the heavens in his work with HARP and was starting to put together the idea of using a massive gun to actually fire satellites into orbit above the Earth.

The design of such a gun was fraught with problems and challenges, but there had been attempts in the past to create guns of enormous size and calibre. In the waning months of World War I, the German Empire deployed a gun used to shell Paris, earning it the name the Paris gun. This artillery piece was 34 metres long and weighed 249 tonnes; it started with a calibre of 211 millimetres before it was rebored to 238 millimetres. The gun had a range of 130 kilometres, several times the range of most other artillery pieces. Its shells were able to reach a height of 42.3 kilometres, which tickled the stratosphere over Earth. It was the first time a human-made object ever reached that kind of altitude. Each shell weighed 234 pounds and reached a speed of 1640 metres per second, meaning each shell took approximately three minutes to reach Paris. It was made with several barrels instead of one long barrel, as most guns were at the time. Unfortunately, the Germans destroyed the gun during the Allied advance that brought the war to an end.

The idea of a supergun was resurrected by the Germans in World War II in the form of the V-3. The weapons came into service beginning in 1944 and were designed to bombard London from bunkers located in the Pas-de Calais region in France. Two similar guns were used to fire at Luxembourg between December 1944 and February 1945. The gun in France was destroyed in an Allied bombing raid before it was completed. The V-3 was again built from multiple barrels that were assembled together. The gun was approximately 130 metres long with a calibre of 150 millimetres and could propel a 310-pound shell to a maximum range of 165 kilometres. Its projected rate of fire was roughly 300 shells per minute, which could have wreaked havoc on London had the gun been brought into service before it was destroyed.

Bull studied both guns in an effort to bring his own dreams to fruition. His initial test results were incredibly promising, so promising in fact, that he needed a larger space to conduct his tests. He managed to secure a surplus 16-inch gun from the U.S. Navy and had it shipped to a test site in Barbados on Foul Bay on the southeast corner of the island. The gun was so large it had be offloaded several miles from its destination and transported there on a railroad line built especially for the purpose of moving the gun. By November 1972, the gun was able to propel a shell to altitudes of 65,500 metres (65.5 kilometres). The shells were equipped to carry equipment that would measure atmospheric conditions. Bull saw this as an opportunity for Canada to get into the space launch business, and he arranged joint funding from both the Canadian government and the U.S. military. He was able to use that funding to build a gun that was 110 feet long.

Bull's guns kept growing in size. In 1966, Bull's launch team set an altitude record for a launched projectile when one of its projectiles reached 189 kilometres. He was running into some problems; however, with his ideas for putting a satellite into space using a large gun. Satellites had extremely sensitive electronics so simply using more propellant to increase the acceleration of the payload was out of the question because the force involved would destroy the electronics. Another issue concerned G-forces and their affect on the payload. Firing a rocket generated a force of roughly three to four Gs. But firing a shell from the barrel of the gun, which rotates the bullet or shell as it passes through the barrel, generated a force of almost 20,000 Gs. Bull hypothesized that a longer gun might be able to generate more acceleration while using less propellant. A larger barrel might also be able to reduce the G-forces inside the barrel.

Bull even started exploring whether or not a large gun could be used to shoot down incoming missiles. But by the late 1960s, the U.S. made it clear that it was more interested in missiles than guns and withdrew its funding from the program. The Canadian government also withdrew funding, even though one of Bull's goals had been to launch a Canadian flag into orbit for the country's centennial in 1967. Bull retreated to his land in Québec, which he was able to reclaim from McGill. He opened up the Space Research Corporation for which he billed himself as an international artillery expert.

Space Research Corporation, despite the title, was clearly in the arms business. He started marketing his services worldwide and found some interest. His first few contracts came from developing nations. Bull was able to produce a package to modify and upgrade old artillery pieces. He was even able to put all of his research and know-how into developing improved artillery pieces and shells. He produced the Gun Canada 45 or GC 45, an improved variation of the 155 millimetre howitzer artillery pieces. The new gun could drop a shell into a 10-metre circle from 30 kilometres away. That range could be boosted to 38 kilometres by sacrificing accuracy, but the range was still approximately double anything NATO had in its inventory at the time. He also developed a new kind of artillery shell that increased the range by almost another 10 kilometres. His first sale, which was auspicious for reasons explained later, was to Israel, to whom he provided 50,000 shells.

The United States, appreciative of all the work Bull had done, rewarded him by making him one of only three people ever granted citizenship by an Act of Congress. The same measure gave Bull a high-level nuclear security clearance. And it appeared that the U.S. was going to do business with Bull, buying his artillery shells. But at the last minute, the U.S. military changed its mind, and Bull was suddenly left with 50,000 shells and no buyer. One player in the U.S. security infrastructure, the CIA, decided to try and help Bull out while also helping itself with one of its strategic objectives.

In 1977, South Africa and its apartheid regime was quickly becoming a pariah of the modern world. The country was engaged in a conflict with Angola, to whom Communist Cuba had sent troops as support. It was one of the many proxy wars playing out across Africa as the United States and Soviet

Union battled for supremacy. South Africa was in need of military equipment, but the United Nations had placed an arms embargo on the country, and the U.S. and Canada also passed laws curtailing arms sales to South Africa.

The CIA offered to try to help broker a deal between South Africa and Bull. The CIA put the two in touch. Bull, now operating out of Brussels, where most arms dealers set up shop, was able to order the 60 gun barrels and 50,000 shells the South Africans needed from a U.S. Army munitions plant. Approval by the U.S. military that should have been months in coming was received in only four days. The 50,000 shells, worth $30 million, were smuggled into South Africa. At the same time, Bull also passed on technology that would allow South Africa to make its own artillery.

Bull quickly found himself being investigated by four different countries. He was even ambushed in a TV interview with British media, who confronted him with the fact that a shipment of arms supposedly intended for Spain had been placed aboard a ship that listed Canada as its destination, but that ship actually travelled to South Africa. Bull, visibly distraught over the accusation, hummed and hawed before saying, "We'll certainly check it."

The U.S. was prepared to bring 15 people to trial for Bull's illegal arms dealing, but on the weekend before the trial, only Bull and one other person went to court. Bull entered a guilty plea, which was allegedly encouraged by the U.S. government as a way to keep evidence of CIA involvement out of court. Bull was shocked when he received a six-month jail sentence instead of the fine he was expecting.

The Canadian arms dealer served his time at the Federal Correction Complex in Allenwood, Pennsylvania. He emerged from prison angry and embittered towards the two countries he felt had betrayed him—the United States and Canada. When he returned to Québec, he was sued and fined $55,000 by the government for his arms dealings.

Bull said in one television interview. "I feel more than betrayed. I feel that all the memories and all the traditions and everything I thought the country stood for has been betrayed. They think they've degraded me. They haven't. They think they've broken my spirit. They haven't. What I did and what I built, to see it cheapened, to see people trying to degrade me personally as a common criminal. For what?"

Set up back in Brussels, Bull turned his back on the West and began working with some questionable countries in an effort to revive his business. He started with Iraq, which in 1981 was still at war with Iran, a conflict that had bogged down with no side generating any clear momentum. He first took a contract with Saddam Hussein's Iraq to upgrade their artillery, but that deal quickly fell apart when it was revealed that Bull was working with China to build a new artillery piece and sell that piece to Iraq.

Bull was able to find lucrative work with China, which meant he was again running afoul of the United States. China wanted artillery with greater range, so Bull signed a three-and-a-half-year contract to engineer a weapon and train the Chinese to manufacture 155 millimetre howitzers, based on his GC 45 design. Bull, however, had not secured a licence from the United States' government to transfer the technology to the Chinese military. The extent of Bull's dealings with China was laid bare on March 23, 1984, when an associate of Bull's was stopped at the U.S. border by Canadian customs officers. The man was carrying a large metal briefcase containing documents, computer disks and contracts. The arms contracts inside were valued at $25 million. But because relations between the U.S. and China were warming, the U.S. took little action.

Eventually, Bull was able to recruit an Austrian steelworks facility named Voest-Alpine to act as his middleman. They bought the licence to his GC 45 gun and started selling it, even negotiating sales to both Iran and Iraq. The U.S. had banned all arms sales to both countries, but Iraq was seen as the favourite of the two in the eyes of the U.S. Saddam was sold on the towed howitzer—an artillery piece that had to be towed by another vehicle—and ordered 200 of the guns. Later that decade, Bull designed two new guns for Saddam Hussein, a self-propelled 155mm howitzer and a self-propelled 210mm howitzer. At the time, the 210 howitzer had the longest range of any gun in the world, at 57 kilometres. The gun also bore a striking resemblance to the G6 artillery piece manufactured in South Africa. Saddam had gone so far as to buy some G6s as well as 200 G5s, which were a direct copy of Bull's GC 45. The guns were capable of firing conventional, biological, chemical and even nuclear weapons.

Bull now had a prestigious, and notorious, client in Saddam Hussein and was able to successfully pitch him his shelved supergun idea. Exactly how he was able to do this is unknown. Bull had always billed his supergun as a peaceful device meant to launch payloads into orbit. But it is believed that Hussein was drawn towards the possible strategic value that such a large gun would bring to his country—a gun that could fire a shell into space could conceivably fire a shell at a target thousands of kilometres away. But as far as anyone knew, using such a gun had serious limitations. It would be difficult, if not impossible, to move and aim the gun at different targets. The rate of fire for such a gun would be slow. In addition, any competent air force could easily destroy the gun because moving it around would be nearly impossible. Still, the thought of being able to easily shell Israel or any other belligerent country in the Middle East may have appealed to Hussein. The Pentagon had passed on the project, so Hussein signed on. Indications are that Bull visited Iraq in 1988, when the two had officially reached a deal.

Bull knew this particular project carried a certain degree of danger, and he did his best to hide his intentions by subcontracting out as many different parts of the gun's construction as possible. He was actually seeking to build two different weapons under Project Babylon. The first, dubbed Baby Babylon, was a 350mm calibre gun that would fire horizontally. Baby Babylon was 46 metres long and weighed 102 tonnes with an expected range of 750 kilometres. The second and larger project was

A section of the Iraqi supergun at Imperial War Museum Duxford

a 1000mm gun, dubbed Big Babylon. This gun would have been 150 metres long and weighed in at 2100 tonnes. With its one-metre bore, the gun would have been capable of launching a 2000-kilogram object into orbit or fire a shell well over 1000 kilometres. Bull cast a wide net looking for supplies, ordering the tubes for the barrels from England, supports for the gun from Greece, the parts for the recoil system from Switzerland and the steel parts for the gun breech from Italy. Altogether, he contracted businesses from eight different countries.

But it was the order for the gunpowder that led to revelations about the true scope of Bull's project. A company in Brussels was tasked with manufacturing the powder. Bull even went so far as to pay the workers at the Brussels factory extra to buy their silence. But the gunpowder's parent company began experiencing financial difficulties and was bought out in 1988 by Astra Defense Systems of Switzerland. When the head of Astra, Dr. John Pike, started looking through the records for the gunpowder factory it had acquired, he was shocked to find some strange contracts. One such contract was for the supply of two different kinds of gunpowder. The contract itself wasn't suspicious. What was suspicious was the sheer size of the pieces of propellant that were ordered. The propellant was being made for two systems, one a 350mm system and the other a 1000mm system. The idea was that the propellant for the 1000mm gun wouldn't be manufactured until the propellant for the 350mm gun had been successfully tested. Indications were that the 350mm gun had been successfully tested in 1989 and that, later that year, an order had been placed for the 1000mm gun.

Bull's work with Saddam was turning him into a marked man. The Iraqi leader was despised throughout the Middle East, and only had favour with the U.S. because of the ongoing tension between Iran and the United States. Hussein was not shy about his hatred for Israel, meaning that anyone working with the Iraqi dictator on any project could be seen as a threat to Israel. Strange things began happening to Bull. He was tailed constantly whenever he was in Europe. His apartment in Brussels was broken into several times, but nothing was ever taken. At one point, Mossad, Israeli's intelligence agency, met with Bull to make it clear that if he continued dealing with Hussein, he was putting his company, his livelihood and his life at risk. Bull even confided in some friends that his life was in danger and that Mossad had threatened him, but he still continued to work with Hussein.

On March 22, 1990, almost two weeks after his 61st birthday, Bull left his office in Brussels to return to his luxury apartment in a chauffeured car. Reports are conflicting on exactly what happened. He was either confronted when he got off the elevator on the sixth floor of the apartment building, where he lived, or when he answered the door of his apartment. Regardless of how it actually happened, Bull was shot and killed, struck by five bullets. Two struck him in the head and three in the back.

Bull's death brought Project Babylon in Iraq to an instant halt. Bull had been the mastermind of the project, and without him, it could not continue. Most of his staff that had been working on the project returned to Canada. It is believed that the smaller test gun was destroyed after the Gulf War ended in 1991.

There are many theories as to who may have killed Bull. The most detailed theory and the most likely is that Mossad, the Israeli intelligence agency, deployed a team to assassinate Bull because of the threat they felt Project Babylon posed to the state. The speculation is certainly plausible since Mossad has a history of kidnapping and even assassinating foreign citizens they feel are a threat. The kidnapping of Nazi Adolf Eichmann from

Argentina to stand trial in Israel in 1960 is perhaps the most famous example, but Mossad has also ordered the assassination of numerous terrorist suspects. Operation Wrath of God, another well-known Mossad operation, was a coordinated effort to track down and kill the architects of and all those believed to have been involved with the slaughter of 11 members of the Israeli Olympic team at the 1972 Olympic Games in Munich. More relevant examples to Bull's case can be found in the steady string of assassinations of Iranian nuclear scientists during the 2000s when Iran was rumoured to be pursuing nuclear weapons technology. So it is not beyond the realm of possibility that Israel's security apparatus saw the development of Project Babylon as a threat and convinced then-Prime Minister Yitzhak Shamir that killing Bull was the only way to disrupt the project. Rumours also circulated that Bull was doing some work on Hussein's SCUD missiles in an effort to make them more robust and useful on the battlefield, which would also have been a threat to Israel.

A *Frontline* documentary on Bull and the supergun, with the help of an Israeli journalist, laid out what it believed was the truth of what happened to Bull. Mossad sent two teams to Brussels to execute Bull. One watched Bull at work, the other waited for him at his apartment building. When Bull left his office, the team watching him clicked its radio once to alert the team at the apartment. When Bull arrived at the apartment building, the team trailing him clicked its radio twice to let them known he had arrived. The team waiting at the apartment building dashed up the stairs to the sixth floor before Bull's elevator got there. When Bull emerged, he was shot five times with a silenced automatic pistol. Both Israeli teams then hopped on the first train they could find, fleeing to Germany before making their way back to Israel. It was also reported that in the days following Bull's death, Mossad helped leak to the European press that Bull had actually been killed by Iraqi agents, who were sent after Bull because he had reneged on his deal with Hussein.

The idea of Iraq killing Bull is not outside the realm of possibility. It is possible that Bull had, in fact, developed a case of cold feet about staying in business with Iraq and Hussein, especially after his alleged meeting with Mossad. Fewer specifics back up this theory, however. Other possible groups that may have been behind his assassination include the CIA because of Bull's earlier dealings with them, and MI6, who had gotten wind of Bull's plans for the supergun. The British eventually seized a shipment of gun barrels, measuring 350 mms and 1000 mms, indicating they knew some details about what was going on.

Other possible suspects include any of the countries with which Bull had done business, such as Chile, South Africa or China. Iran had just as much of a motive to want Bull dead as Israel, but Iran's intelligence resources were seen as less capable than Israel's at the time. The only thing certain is that Bull's killing was not a robbery gone wrong. Several reports indicate that at the time of his death, Bull was carrying $20,000 in cash in his pocket, and the money was found with his body.

Bull was laid to rest in Québec, his funeral attended by several hundred people. The gun he had been working on in Iraq was dismantled, though parts of it were later found on display at one of Saddam Hussein's properties following the American invasion and liberation of Iraq in 2003. Bull did leave a much more immediate and deadly legacy to the Middle East. Three months after his death, Saddam Hussein ordered the invasion of Kuwait. However, a coalition of countries from across the world united in Saudi Arabia to drive the Iraqis out of Kuwait. When the ground campaign for Operation Desert Storm began and coalition troops crossed over to start fighting the Iraq army, several hundred of the artillery pieces the Iraqi army deployed to fight the coalition had been created by none other than Gerald Bull.

Bull's story lived on far past his death. In 1994, HBO aired a TV movie about his life and death entitled *The Doomsday Gun*. Bull also made an appearance as a character in the Frederick Forsyth novel, *The Fist of God*. In the story, Bull believes his gun is being built to launch Arab satellites into space, but he is killed by the Iraqis when he realizes Hussein's true intentions to use it to fire a nuclear weapon. The plot of the book revolves around the coalition's attempt to destroy the weapon before it can be used. Bull's story was also adapted for the theatre. Entitled *Three in the Back, Two in the Chest,* the play focuses on a fictional scientist named Donald Jackson, who has developed a missile defence system and is killed by the CIA. Jackson's character was based on Gerald Bull.

Regardless of the information that has found its way into the public domain, no one has ever been charged with Bull's murder. It is highly unlikely that anyone ever will be.

The Man Called Intrepid

~

William Stephenson (1897–1989) might be one of Canada's most mysterious citizens. The man grew to be an important person in the world of espionage during World War II. However, it was later discovered that some of his story was fabricated as a result of some rather liberal creative license taken. While the actual details are far less interesting than those initially published, Stephenson's contributions to the war effort cannot be ignored.

Born in Manitoba, Stephenson enlisted to serve in World War I. He became a pilot but was shot down and held prisoner. He later escaped, taking with him a unique kind of can opener that he hoped to patent back home. The can opener wasn't a success, but Stephenson soon found success in other business ventures overseas. When World War II broke out, Stephenson was tasked as the head of an organization called British Security Coordination (BSC), which was set up in the United States. BSC's mission was to try to learn as much as possible about possible Axis operations in North America and to try and bring the United States into the war. BSC engaged in an extensive, and highly illegal, mail-opening operation to look for secret messages written in invisible ink or using microdots. It conducted intelligence operations designed to deter the activities of Nazi Germany. Stephenson was also responsible for founding Camp X in Canada, a school where Allied intelligence operatives trained.

BSC's activities ended when the war ended. A series of books introduced Stephenson to the broader public but some, including *A Man Called Intrepid*, exaggerated some of his activities during the war. He is also considered by some to be the inspiration for Ian Fleming's James Bond. But as secretive as he was in life, Stephenson even tried to conceal his death. He left instructions that after he died (in 1989) that news of his death be withheld from the press until after his body was buried.

Chapter 10

Peter Verigin

~

Immigration helped build Canada into the strong, prosperous country it is today. Canada's model of multiculturalism encourages immigrant communities to maintain their own identity while fully participating in their new home country. At the beginning of the 20th century, Canada was seen as something of a blank canvas for many immigrant groups, a land where they might be free of the oppression they had experienced in their home countries and where tracts of thousands of acres land were just waiting to be settled. But some of those groups, intentionally or not, brought trouble with them, either in the form of internal conflicts or that developed over time or by offending the Canadian communities with which they attempted to live peacefully. In at least one of those cases, though it is not known exactly who committed the crime, that conflict produced a deadly result.

Most Canadians are somewhat familiar with the Doukhobors, a religious community of Europeans that immigrated to Canada in the early part of the 20th century. Their community and way of life was born in southern Russia in the 18th century. But the Doukhobors beliefs brought the community into conflict with the Russian Orthodox Church. They rejected the church's focus on icons of religious figures, likening it to idol worship. The Doukhobors came to believe that each person contained a "spark of God" within themselves, meaning that every person was equal and that taking a human life, in any context, was akin to killing God. So the Doukhobors believed in pacifism. They also believed in communal living and emphasized oral psalms and songs over the physical bible.

They were originally referred to as Dukho-borets, a phrase coined by the Russian Orthodox Church that branded the group as heretics who "struggled against holy spirits." The group, however, adopted the term to mean that they were true "spirit wrestlers or holy people." As a result of being branded heretics by the mainstream church in Russia, the community faced political and religious persecution. In the early part of the 19th century the group was forcibly relocated to the territories bordering the Russian Empire. They were eventually relocated twice more, finally being left in the mountainous Caucasus area between the Black and Caspian Seas.

The Doukhobors had their own religious leaders. In 1864, that person was a man named Peter Kalmykov, but Kalmykov died that year, leaving his widow Lukeria Gubanova in his place as leader. By the 1880s, Lukeria wished to designate someone as a possible successor, one of the cousins of Peter Kalmykov, a young man named Peter Verigin.

Verigin was born on July 12, 1859, in the village of Slavyanka in the Elisabetpol Governorate of the Russian Empire, located just to the northwest of what is present-day Azerbaijan. His father, Vasiliy was illiterate but a relatively well-off peasant who had once been elected the leader of his village. Peter was one seven sons. The four older boys received no education, but Peter and his brothers Vasiliy and Grigory were home-schooled to read and write. In either 1879 or 1882, Peter married a young woman named Evdokia Georgievna Kotelnikova. That same year, he started working as an assistant to Lukeria Guba-nova, the new leader of the Transcaucasian Doukhobors.

Lukeria saw promise in the young man and took him into her home to give him a religious education and to prepare him to be the future leader of the Doukhobors. She soon discovered that Peter was already married and insisted that the marriage be annulled. Peter agreed.

In 1886, Lukeria died, and a struggle over the leadership of the Doukhobors ensued. In a January 1887 meeting, a majority of the Doukhobors selected Peter as their leader. But a great division emerged in the community. Those who supported Peter were called the Large Party, while those who wanted Lukeria's brother Michal Gubanova to be leader were called the Small Party. While Peter was the choice of the majority, the Small Party had greater political connections. They convinced Czarist officials that Verigin was a threat to the government, and in 1887, Peter was arrested and sent to live in internal exile.

He was moved around, first living in Sheknursk in the north before being transferred in 1890 to Kola, on the Barents Sea. In November 1894, he was moved again, this time to Obdorsk in northern Siberia. Yet despite his exile, Peter stayed in contact with his people by writing letters. During his exile, he read extensively, and much of what he read influenced the directions he gave to his followers in letters to them. He adopted vegetarianism and asked his people to adopt it as well, also imploring them to abstain from the use of alcohol and tobacco. He re-emphasized the Doukhobors commitment to pacifism, reminding them of the commandment, "Thou shalt not kill." This particular direction manifested itself in on the night June 28, 1895, when Doukhobors in three different villages burned all the weapons they owned, a move that instantly brought violent reprisals from government Cossacks.

But the plight of the Doukhobors was growing in the public eye. Even Leo Tolstoy, the famous author, learned of their circumstances and tried to do something to improve their lives. The Doukhobors had heard of Canada and considered the prospect of moving to a new land where they might be able to live peacefully and relatively undisturbed. Verigin went so far as to write a letter to Empress Alexandra, wife of Czar Nicholas, suggesting a few different proposals to resolve the state of conflict between the Empire and the Doukhobors. One of those proposals was that the Czar allow the Doukhobors to leave Russia for Canada.

Peter V. Verigin, known as Peter the Lordly

In 1898, an agreement was reached between the Doukhobor community and the Czar that would allow for the Doukhobors to emigrate. Over the next year, roughly 7500 Doukhobors made the voyage across the Atlantic to Canada, but Verigin had not yet been released from his government exile. In the interim, his people settled in Saskatchewan and accumulated a significant amount of land, living communally and trying to live Verigin's mantra of "toil and peaceful life."

It was not until December 1902 that Verigin, now referred to by many of his followers as Lordly, was released from custody and left Russia for Canada. His arrival came at an auspicious time. His people were already starting to generate enmity with their neighbours, and the hope was that Verigin's arrival might tame the conflict. But news of his journey to Canada motivated thousands of his followers to march en masse across Canada to meet him. They were finally stopped in Manitoba and sent on trains back to their home. Verigin eventually did arrive, and when he did, the Doukhobors celebrated. They renamed the village they had founded from "Poterpevshie," which translates as either "The Victims" or "The Survivors," to "Otradnove," which meant "The Place of Rejoicing."

The community served as Verigin's headquarters until around 1904 when the Canadian Northern Railway crossed within 10 kilometres of the village. A small station was built beside the tracks to allow access for the Doukhobors, and the community subsequently established itself there, calling itself Veregin. Peter moved his headquarters to that town.

It didn't take long before the Doukhobors found themselves in conflict with the Canadian federal government. In 1903, 50 members of the community tried to recreate the march they had begun when Verigin arrived in the country, only this time most of the participants decided to do the march naked. They were stopped by the authorities outside Yorkton, forcibly dressed and imprisoned.

Doukhobor village near Veregin, SK, 50 kilometres northeast of Yorkton

In 1905, the government passed its Dominion Lands Act, and in so doing tried to get the Doukhobors to register their land under individual ownership. However, because the Doukhobors believed in communal living, they refused to have any of their land registered under any one person's name. The Doukhobors also refused to become naturalized citizens because doing so would require them to swear an oath of allegiance to the Crown, which they refused to do. The tension reached such a high point that Verigin, in 1906, returned to Russia to investigate the possibility of the Doukhobors returning to their homeland. The revolution of 1905 had taken place, and Verigin wondered if the changes that stemmed from the revolution might make Russia a more peaceful place for the Doukhobors to live. While he was away, however, the government officially abolished the communal land system and seized 650,000 of the Doukhobors' 773,000 acres of land. When Verigin returned, rather than stay in Saskatchewan and tend the property they had been given, he moved all of his people to a 15,000-acre site in BC. Verigin liked the climate in BC and believed he could easily add more land to the Doukhobors holdings.

Over the next five years, some 5000 followers moved to the new community in BC, and they prospered. Besides farming, the Doukhobors built sawmills, a brick-making plant and a jam factory. Some people stayed behind in Saskatchewan, and Peter found himself now forced to travel between the communities of his followers. In order to do so efficiently, Verigin started taking the train to the different destinations. It was this move that would increasingly bring him into conflict with a traditional sect that had formed within his own followers. They were called the *svobodniki* or Freedomites.

The Freedomites, who had featured prominently in the attempted nude march of 1903, were traditionalists who believed that using any modern conveniences went against the lifestyle of the Doukhobors. They had already caused some problems in Saskatchewan, where they were suspected to have burned some modern farm equipment. When they heard that Verigin was now taking the train to visit the various communities, they were infuriated. At one point, Verigin expelled all the Freedomites from the community as a whole, but still permitted them to squat on Doukhobor land. The group was even suspected of once burning down Verigin's communal home.

Doukhobor women near Verigin, Saskatchewan

Verigin preaching among his followers in 1923 in British Columbia

The Doukhobors were also finding themselves increasingly in conflict with the population and government of BC. First, the people who lived close to the Doukhobors were critical of the impact their operation had on local businesses. The communal villages had a seemingly endless supply of manpower with which few other businesses in the area could compete. Tension also mounted between the provincial government and the Doukhobors over the issue of education for the Doukhobors' children. The government believed that the children should be required to attend school, while the Doukhobors disagreed, thinking they should be able to educate their children however they saw fit. The government saw public education as a way to transform new immigrants to the country into good Canadian citizens. To the Doukhobors, the only purpose of an education was to prepare their children to work in the home or in their fields. The Doukhobors responded to this conflict with varying levels of protest, ranging from nude demonstrations at schools and even allegedly burning some schools. Conflict further sharpened during the outbreak of World War I, when the Doukhobors pacifist beliefs brought them into conflict with those Canadians who believed that serving the British Empire overseas in the war was an important duty.

As time went on, and the conflict over the Doukhobors and schools continued, the government began imposing fines on the community. When the Doukhobors did not pay the fines, the government ordered raids of their properties, seizing equipment that was intended to cover the cost of the fines. Some members of the community were even jailed as a result of the ongoing conflict over schooling.

This was the lay of Peter Verigin's land on October 28, 1924, when he boarded a Canadian Pacific Railway Train. The train was travelling on the Kettle Valley Line. It had just passed Farron, located between Castlegar and Grand Forks. Around 1:00 AM, an explosion tore through car 1586, the same car Verigin was travelling in. The force of the explosion ripped the passenger car apart, throwing bodies onto the ground outside the car. The train's engineers and workers did what they could to help the wounded and cut the burning car loose from the train. They transferred the injured to a sleeper car and headed back to Castlegar under the direction of the brakeman. Two of the injured died on the journey to Castlegar.

The location of the incident proved to be a problem for investigators to reach because it was an isolated line. The nearest station, Farron, was a minor station in the Monashee Mountains. It was mostly used for crew and equipment changes, and there were no roads leading to the area where the blast took place. That meant a special train had to be chartered for some, while others reached the area by handcar. Within days, the full death toll from the explosion had been settled. Nine individuals travelling in the passenger car had died, among them Peter Verigin. His body was found on the ground outside the passenger train. One leg had been severed in the blast.

Word of the explosion quickly made the news in BC, even nationally, and the initial reports all pointed to some kind of accident. A large tank of gas had been carried underneath the car, the gas being used to light the lamps in the coach. It was initially reported that some kind of accident ignited this fuel, causing the explosion. However, reports from the train employees stated that, after they stopped the train following the explosion, the tanks beneath the passenger car were the first thing they checked. They were intact. The investigators started looking at the possibility of some kind of deliberately planted explosive or "infernal device" as the cause.

"This indicates that the explosion was caused by some agency inside the car entirely other than any part of the equipment," read one investigator's report.

Two coroner's inquires were quickly initiated. One inquiry, in Grand Forks, constituted itself only 19 hours after the explosion and began investigating the deaths of Peter Verigin, John McKie, Haakum Singh and Peter J. Campbell. Down the line, a second inquest began its sitting on November 1 to examine what had caused the deaths of Harry Bishop, Neil Murry and Mary Strelaeff. Two passengers injured in the blast died after the inquests had already been struck but no further inquiry was held for them. The presence of Mary Strelaeff's body would later prove important because she was a 17-year-old who had been travelling with Verigin at the time of the explosion. Besides Verigin, one other prominent person travelling aboard the train had died. John McKie was a member of the BC legislature, representing Grand Forks-Greenwood. He was a Conservative, and at the time of the blast, he was travelling to Victoria to take his seat in the legislature after the most recent election.

If a train exploded today, a veritable army of investigators from several different agencies would descend on the site and likely spend weeks examining the scene and combing the area for evidence. In the 1920s, neither sufficient resources nor the necessary scientific techniques were available to mount such a comprehensive investigation. In total, maybe a dozen investigators worked on the case, including those from the RCMP, the BC provincial police and the CPR's own investigators. Those dozen investigators spent only a day or two at the scene, examining the evidence they could find. What they did find seemed to lend credence to the emerging theory that a bomb or an explosive had caused the blast. They marked the positions of the bodies that were found outside the passenger car. They retrieved from the area a dry cell battery that appeared to have strange connections soldered to it. They also found the remains of a clock in the area, a clock that was later determined to be of Italian manufacture. The fact that the passenger car was the only car on the train affected by the explosion also pointed to the possibility that someone on board had been the target of the bomb.

"We know it must have been caused by a high explosive, but that is almost all we know so far," one Staff Sergeant Gammon was quoted as saying.

There was nothing else remarkable about the train itself. The train consisted of an engine, a tender, a café car, a mail car and a baggage car, along with the day passenger car that had exploded. At the time of the explosion, 21 people were travelling in the day passenger car. It had a capacity of 75 people. The explosion, it appeared, had taken place in the centre of the car.

"From splinters on the track below where the coach had been at the time would confirm the belief that some form of dynamite had exploded within the coach," said a report in the *Nelson Daily News*. "So terrific was the explosion that more than half of the passengers were blown clear of the car and left a gruesome spectacle of mutilated humanity and wreckage for nearly 10 feet."

Only one body was found inside the car; the rest had been blown clear. Verigin's body was found on the north side of the coach, his head facing the railroad tracks, 4 to 6 metres from John McKie's body, which had been blown 15 metres from the passenger car. Another body found nearby had been "mutilated beyond recognition." Upon further examination, the investigators found the presence of the battery cell peculiar, especially because of how it had been modified. Something believed to be a piece of tin was soldered or somehow connected to one part of the battery, and a coppery cap was found attached to the opposite terminal. Investigators did not find any evidence that such a battery was used in any of the train equipment. Experts who examined the battery believed it was actually a kind of medical battery, but such a battery properly used would have copper connections at its terminals, not the tin found soldered to the top.

Reports from the RCMP showed that they believed the explosion had taken place directly over the tanks containing the gas for the coach's lamps. But further examination of the tanks found that, while dented, they were not compromised enough to have blown up. The force of the explosion; however, had blown a hole in the floor of the coach and even snapped one of the railroad ties over which the train had been travelling.

As for the clock, the police first examined the possibility that it may have come from the baggage of one of the passengers. Nando Singh, who had been travelling with his brother, was reported to have been carrying a large alarm clock and a watch in his suitcase, but neither was found to contain the kinds of parts the police found at the scene.

Interviews with people operating the train at the time of the explosion helped construct a more accurate picture about what had happened. According to the engineers and brakemen, the train had been travelling at approximately 30 kilometres per hour when the explosion occurred. The engineer, William Harkness, said the train's emergency brakes automatically engaged after the blast. He and one of the brakemen ran towards the coach once the train stopped to try and help the people inside escape. While they were helping the others, Harkness told investigators that he had heard some smaller explosions, "like dynamite caps or small cartridges exploding." He quickly bent down to check the gas tanks under the car and found them still attached. He then ordered the passenger car cut away from the rest of the train for safety.

Some passengers reported a couple of suspicious-looking characters hanging around one of the stations before the train's stop in Farron, and that one of those individuals had boarded the train. The conductor told investigators it was entirely possible for someone to board the train and then hop off without any workers on the train noticing.

A report taken in 1931 seemed to point a finger of suspicion at someone who might have done just this. Archibald Joseph Blaney claimed in his statement that two Doukhobor men had boarded the train at Castlegar and that each of them was carrying a suitcase. The men placed their suitcases close to where Peter Verigin was sitting, had a brief conversation with him, shook his hand and then left the train. Blaney himself left the train at Farron, before the explosion, which may explain why it took so many years for him to provide any kind of statement.

The inquests sitting in both communities didn't have access to Blaney's information at the time. However, both came to the independent conclusions that all those who died had perished because of the explosion, which had been deliberately set. And while the inquests didn't assign blame to any one person or party, it was believed that whoever set the bomb was targeting Peter Verigin.

The Doukhobors at first did not believe that anyone had deliberately placed a bomb on board; they felt that the entire ordeal had been an accident. The Doukhobors chartered a special train from Nelson to Farron to recover Verigin's body. He was buried at Brilliant, just outside Castlegar. However, the Doukhobors' belief that the explosion was accidental quickly changed to an inference that he had been deliberately assassinated.

They came to believe the account of one of the Doukhobors travelling with Verigin, who had been sitting on the other side of the coach. This person had seen something peculiar. Apparently at one point in the journey, Verigin's companion, one Masha Grigovrena Astaforoff, noticed the conductor walk through the passenger car, holding some kind of object. He began waving it around. The stick was described as "such a stick I saw in the hands of doctors when performing operations." Shortly after the conductor started waving the stick around in the air, everyone on board the car began falling asleep. Astaforoff said she was able to fight the impulse to sleep at first and that she saw someone approach Verigin, lean in close to see if he was asleep, then place a small suitcase underneath his seat. The substance that was being discharged into the air was believed to be chloroform. After the explosion, Astaforoff escaped the car and was standing on the side of the tracks when she saw the conductors running around then stopping at a point near where Verigin's body was later found. They began striking something.

> *Then it was I guessed, they were searching for* [Verigin] *and when finding him, probably saw that he was still alive, and to be sure he died, were finishing him off.*

> *Praise the Lord! The Holy Prophet Petushka the Lordly was killed by the authorities of the Canadian law in a spirit of enmity, under the heavens.*

The Doukhobors later wrote an open letter to the BC government accusing them of killing Verigin:

> *In my opinion as well as the members of our community you have ravished our great wrestler.*

Many who believed that Verigin was the target speculated that it was neither the Canadian nor BC governments that targeted him but a sect within the Doukhobor community, possibly the Freedomites. Given that Verigin had clashed with them earlier and effectively exiled them from the community, it was logical to suspect the spin-off group of having deliberately planted the bomb on board the train in order to get rid of Verigin. The police followed this particular lead the most and had, after interviewing several people, begun looking for two Russian individuals. They had reports that one witness had seen an individual, either a Doukhobor or a Russian, get on the train at Brilliant around the same time that Verigin boarded the train. That person then disembarked at Castlegar.

The first was more a shadow than a person, a watchmaker named Metro Grishin who went by several different aliases. The second was a much more memorable character, a man by the name of Sam Kamenshikoff, who was a Doukhobor often in conflict with Verigin. Verigin had exiled Kamenshikoff and some of his followers. The two had even gotten into a physical fight two months before the bombing, and those interviewed said that Verigin had beaten Kamenshikoff quite handily. Kamenshikoff was most memorable for his peculiar form of dress. He was known as "Orange Sam" because he liked to wear a crown of 21 oranges. The number of oranges in the crown was deliberate; he saw them as representing three meals a day for a week. He said they also represented God and would serve as food for Jesus Christ during his second coming. The police went so far as arrest and jail Orange Sam for a time before releasing him without charge.

Still others were suspected of assassinating Verigin. His wife, Anastasia Holubova, was even suspected. The two had been married for quite some time, but recently Verigin had been travelling with Mary Strelaeff, a 17-year-old follower. Strelaeff was described as Verigin's secretary, but that seemed suspicious since Doukhobor women were not generally taught to read and write. It may have been that Anastasia suspected an affair between Verigin and Strelaeff and tried to kill one or both of them. No direct evidence supports this theory.

Another possible conspirator was the Soviet government. The October Revolution of 1917 replaced the Provisional Government with the Bolsheviks, who were now trying to build a Communist utopia under Vladimir Lenin. While Lenin had died before Verigin, it was believed that the Soviets looked favourably upon the Doukhobors returning to Russia. Their communal lifestyle as well as their knowledge of modern farming methods would have been welcome in a Communist regime. Verigin opposed such a return, believing the Soviets should get rid of all military conscription and declare the Soviet Union as a perpetually neutral country in all affairs. It's possible that the Soviets might have seen killing Verigin as a way to get the Doukhobors to return. If they killed the leader who opposed their return, the rest might choose to come back under a new leader.

There were other suggestions that the Ku Klux Klan may have been involved. Verigin had recently travelled to Oregon where he purchased some land, raising the prospect of a Doukhobor migration to the United States. The KKK was active in Oregon at the time. Others believe it may have been someone from a nearby community who was incensed by the problems the Doukhobors were causing with respect to schooling and children, as well as their propensity for protesting in the nude. Some even saw the Doukhobors as Bolsheviks, given their refusal to fight in the army during World War I, their communal lifestyle and their Russian origins.

The entire incident may have simply been a part of a struggle for total power and authority over the Doukhobors. After Peter died, the community had to choose a new leader. The contest pitted Verigin's widow, Anastasia, against Verigin's son from his first marriage, Peter P. Verigin.

One of the most thorough independent investigations undertaken actually unearthed evidence that implicated Peter P. It was a book, *Terror in the Name of God: The Story of the Sons of Freedom Doukhobors*, written by journalist Simma Holt in 1964 that made the connection. Peter P. had been raised in Russia and was still living there when he was selected as leader by a majority of the Doukhobors in Canada. He came to Canada once in 1906 to see his father and apparently became quite embittered toward his father for abandoning his mother and becoming so successful. So it may have been, the book suggested, that Peter P. arranged to have Verigin killed so that

Peter P. could take his place. In the end, Peter P. was selected as the next leader of the Doukhobors, and Anastasia left the community with 500 of her own followers before Peter P. arrived in Canada. His return was delayed when the Russian authorities arrested him for drunkenness and assault before he could leave.

Peter P.'s reign led to the ruin of the Doukhobors. He was a violent drunk who gambled away the commune's money during his 12-year rule. In 1938, the Doukhobors were forced as an entity to declare bankruptcy. The RCMP, once Holt's book came out, conducted interviews to explore Holt's theory a little more, but nothing came of it.

One last theory suggests that another person on the train might have been the target of the bomb, and not Peter Verigin at all. One of the other passengers on the train was John McKie, member of the legislature for Grand Forks-Greenwood. McKie was a Conservative. In the most recent election, the Liberals, under John Oliver had emerged with a plurality of 24 of 48 possible seats in the BC legislature. The Conservatives won 18 seats, the Provincials three seats and Labour won three seats as well, meaning that the opposition had in total as many seats as the Liberals. And the legislature had yet to select a Speaker for the legislature, which would likely have come from the Liberals. Since the Speaker doesn't vote in the legislature, the Liberals would have been left with only 23 seats, compared to 24 seats total for the opposition, giving rise to a minority government for Oliver. It was suggested that by eliminating McKie, the Conservatives lost one seat, as it would have been declared vacant. So if the Speaker was selected from the Liberals, and they had only 23 votes in the legislature, the opposition would have only 23 seats as well. In fact, Oliver's Liberals went on to serve an entire four-year term, and even though he lost his own seat in the election, Oliver stayed on as premier until 1927.

No one has ever been charged in the death of Peter Verigin. One year after his death, his body was moved to a new tomb. The tomb was bombed twice. No one knows by whom.

Who Discovered the West Coast of Canada First?

~

For some reason, the discovery of the West Coast by Europeans is a little more obscure than the discovery of the East Coast. Some contend that the Spaniards may have passed through during the 1600s, but no real proof supports the theory. Although Spaniard Vasco Núñez de Balboa, did reach the West Coast of the Americas through Panama and claim all lands bordering on the Pacific Ocean for Spain.

It is widely believed that Juan Perez from Spain first visited Vancouver Island and the Queen Charlotte Islands in the late 18th century, most likely in 1774. There were more visits in later years by the Americans, the Spanish and the British. There is also some evidence of Russian fur-trading settlements along the coast of North America dating back to the 1700s. However, it was seafaring Captain James Cooke and subsequently Captain George Vancouver of the British Royal Navy who in the late 1700s finally went to the trouble of surveying the West Coast and claiming the land for England.

~

Chapter 11

Harry Oakes

~

People who roll their eyes and complain about how frequently the behaviours and tragedies of celebrities and other famous people end up in the news should take some solace in the fact that this isn't a recent phenomenon. The antics of the rich and famous have been driving the legitimate problems of the world off the front pages of newspapers for hundreds of years. And one unsolved celebrity murder has a prominent Canadian connection. It was seen as so scandalous that it even successfully displaced news about World War II on the front pages of newspapers across the world. It was the story of Sir Harry Oakes.

Those who live in Ontario are likely familiar with the Oakes name, even if they don't necessarily know where it comes from. Oakes Park is in Niagara Falls, and when completed in 1931, it was a top of the line athletic facility with a baseball stadium, two smaller baseball fields, a soccer pitch as well as a 400-metre athletics track, and some of those same amenities exist to this day. The Oakes Garden Theatre, opened in September 1937, was built on land donated by Harry Oakes to the

Niagara Parks Commission, of which he was a member. But while Oakes planted some of his roots solidly in Canada, he was actually born in the United States and died in the Bahamas under peculiar circumstances. Still, for all intents and purposes, his business dealings in Canada sent him to the Bahamas in the first place.

～

Harry Oakes was born December 23, 1874, in Sangerville, Maine, to William and Edith Oakes. William was a successful lawyer and subsequently could afford a private education

Harry and Eunice Oakes in Toronto, sometime in the 1930s

～

for his children. His parents sent Harry to the Foxcroft Academy, and he eventually enrolled at Bowdoin College in 1896. He then spent two years at Syracuse University Medical School, but in 1898, Oakes, like many others of his time, caught gold fever and made his way north at the height of the Klondike gold rush. He was more interested in making his fortune as a prospector than he was in being a doctor. He spent the next 15 years looking for gold around the world in places such as Australia and California. Finally, in 1912, after searching for more than a decade, Oakes finally struck gold, this time in Canada. His find was a massive gold reserve at Kirkland Lake in Northern Ontario. He established Lake Shore Mine to operate the mine, which within 20 years was one of the most productive gold mines in the world and ranked as the second-largest gold mine in the Americas. By 1920, Oakes was Canada's richest person.

He decided to celebrate his success in 1923 by taking a world cruise, and when the ship docked in Australia, be met the love of his life, Eunice Myrtle McIntyre, who was living in Sydney. The two were married on June 30, 1923. People took notice of the marriage, as Eunice was less than half Oakes' age at the time. She was 22, while Harry was 48. Their first child, Nancy, was born in 1924, and they went on to have five children, with two years separating each child.

The two returned to Canada, and in 1924, moved to Niagara Falls. Harry built a 35-room mansion on a 20-acre estate on Clark Hill. The mansion had 17 bathrooms, air conditioning and featured a swimming pool and a five-hole golf course (Oakes was an avid golfer). When the stock market crashed and the Great Depression came, Oakes was able to continue building his fortune. He even started creating make-work projects for others less fortunate. He created jobs by restoring roads and paying $2.00 for a half-day's work, always rotating shifts so that as many people who wanted to could work. In September 1930, he deeded 16 acres of farmland for an athletics park that was called Oakes Park. It opened in 1931. He also contributed the land to the Niagara Parks Commission for the Oakes Garden Theatre and was rewarded with a seat on the commission.

But Harry Oakes, like most wealthy individuals, was mostly concerned with making more money and keeping the money he had already made. And the Canadian government was trying to take as much of his money in taxes as possible. Calculations available today showed that he was paying more than $3 million in taxes a year, which he used to say worked out to $17,500 a day. The government wanted as much as 85 per cent of his wealth in taxes, and was taxing his mine so heavily that the taxes worked out to 25 per cent of the gold mined there.

So instead of staying in Canada, in 1935, Harry moved south to the Bahamas, where he was openly received as someone who could help better develop the area. He already had a friend there named Harold Christie, a real estate developer who helped convince Oakes to move his family and his money to the area. Within four years of arriving in Nassau, Oakes was rewarded with a baronetcy for his philanthropic work in Canada and the Bahamas, and for donations he made to a hospital in London.

He soon became a major business player in the Bahamas, working as an investor, entrepreneur and land developer. He played a role in expanding the airport in Nassau, the capital; he built a golf course and country club there as well as new housing. His projects helped stimulate the economy, which, like all other economies in the West, were struggling mightily at the time. It was estimated at one time that Oakes alone owned one-third of the island of New Providence.

On the evening of July 7, 1943, Oakes went to bed in his Nassau mansion. His wife was back in the United States at their summer home in Vermont, but Oakes wasn't alone in the house. Harold Christie had been visiting Oakes for a few days and was spending the night in a room just down the hall from Oakes' bedroom. When Christie awoke on the morning of July 8, he walked into Oakes' bedroom and found his friend dead.

He had obviously been murdered. Oakes was beaten to death, and someone had strewn the bed with feathers from a pillow and tried to set the bed on fire. However, an enormous storm that had walloped Nassau the night before appeared to have blown out the fire. Closer examination found that death had come from a blow to the head from an object that was believed to be a club with protruding spikes. The accelerant used to start the fire was determined to be either petrol or gasoline. When the police arrived, one of the first people they interviewed was Christie, who asserted that, besides waking up to swat a few mosquitoes, he hadn't heard anything, even the massive storm that had blown so hard that it had extinguished the fire in Oakes' bedroom.

The Governor General of the Bahamas was unnerved by the murder of Harry Oakes, who was a close friend. The Governor General was not new to controversy. While he was currently known as the Duke of Windsor, he had, in a previous life, been known as King Edward VII of England. He had ruled England for exactly 326 days in 1936 before abdicating. Edward's relationship with a divorced woman, Wallis Simpson, touched off a constitutional crisis over whether or not the King, as head of the Church of England, could marry a divorced person. At the time, the church opposed the remarriage of divorced people whose former spouses were still alive. Edward abdicated the throne, and was succeeded by his brother Albert, who became known was King George VI. Edward was then named the Duke of Windsor. He married Simpson in France in June 1937 after her second divorce was finalized and then was assigned to the Bahamas as Governor General.

The Duke did not want a media scandal, and at first tried his best to silence any media coverage of Harry's murder. He was also, for reasons never fully explained, nervous about letting the authorities in Nassau investigate the murder. Rather than let them, he sent to the United States for a pair of police officers from Miami who had worked on the Duke's private security team during some of his earlier trips to the U.S. Those detectives were Edward Melchen and James Barker; they flew to Nassau within 24 hours of receiving the Duke's request.

The two detectives interviewed Harold Christie, who maintained that he hadn't left the house, that he had slept soundly and that he hadn't heard anything suspicious during the night, even though his room was only two doors down from Oakes. But while Christie's story might have seemed suspicious, the detectives already seemed to have a suspect in mind—Count Alfred de Marigny, who was married to Oakes' daughter Nancy.

Oakes and de Marigny didn't get along. Nancy and de Marigny had eloped in 1942, two days before her 19th birthday. They met at a Nassau Yacht Club and had been dating for a couple of years. He had been married twice before to wealthy women and was seen as something of a playboy with no meaningful career. He did not ask Oakes' permission to marry Nancy, and the two men were seen to argue more than once. Nancy was also due, upon Oakes' death, to inherit a sizeable part of his fortune. But it appeared that de Marigny had a bit of an alibi. That evening he had hosted a dinner party, and had even personally driven many of his guests home afterwards. They did establish, however, that there was a 30-minute window of time in which de Marigny could not account for his whereabouts.

When the detectives interrogated de Marigny, they asked him to pour a glass of water and handed him a fresh pack of cigarettes that had not yet been opened. Suddenly, without warning, the Duke of Windsor showed up, spoke privately with the two detectives for about 20 minutes then left. No one knows what was said, but two hours later, de Marigny was arrested and charged with the murder of his father-in-law, Sir Harry Oakes. One of the most telling pieces of evidence was a perfect, unsmudged fingerprint matching de Marigny's prints that the detectives said they pulled from a screen in Oakes' bedroom.

Nancy refused to believe her husband could have committed the murder and helped to mount a vigorous defence for him. She eventually made her way to Nassau and hired prominent lawyer Godfrey W. Higgs and a private investigator to look into the case. Higgs was, however, looking at a challenging case. The authorities were so convinced of de Marigny's guilt that it was reported they'd already ordered the rope that would be used to hang him.

But it was the fingerprint meant to prove de Marigny's guilt that would help him achieve acquittal. Barker apparently told Oakes' widow and Nancy only one day after Oakes' funeral that they knew de Marigny was the killer because they had found a fingerprint belonging to him in the bedroom. Yet upon cross-examination, Barker said it had actually taken several more days for them to identify the print, and that he had taken several dozen other prints from the room that, after several weeks passed, still hadn't been processed. The print had been lifted perfectly and cleanly and did not include any of the material from the screen on which it had been allegedly found, an almost impossible feat. When asked in court to recreate how he had so perfectly lifted the print from the screen, he was unable to do so.

There was also the issue of the photo of the print. Most of the prints that were revealed by the fingerprint powder were photographed before they were lifted, so the photos showed the surfaces on which they were found. Other prints on the screen had been photographed to show where on the screen they had been found. But the screen was not visible in the photograph of de Marigny's print. It was believed that the detectives lifted de Marigny's print from either the water glass he used during his interrogation or the cellophane around the cigarette pack they offered him, and then they placed the print on the screen.

There were other parts of the trial that, in hindsight, should have cast a great deal of doubt on de Marigny's guilt. The Duke of Windsor, who had gone to such great lengths to hush up the investigation and bring in two American police officers, somehow managed to be in the United States when the trial for the murder of one of his friends got underway. The Duke himself was never questioned, nor was he ever interrogated about the private conversation shared with the two American detectives. It is believed that neither detective would have planted de Marigny's fingerprint without receiving explicit direction from the duke.

There was also the issue of Christie who, when called to the stand, maintained that he heard absolutely nothing that night even though he slept only two doors down from Oakes. During his testimony, Christie appeared nervous, tired and uncertain. He began to sweat profusely and had to dab his forehead with a handkerchief. He maintained he only woke up to swat a few mosquitoes and that the ferocious thunderstorm hadn't woke him up at all. When asked how implausible that sounded, Christie replied that it might sound implausible, but it was still true.

Nancy also gave a vigorous defence of her husband on the stand. She appeared in court almost every single day and even appeared to come close to fainting while giving her own testimony.

The judge in the case took five hours to charge jury with their instructions. They returned two hours later with their verdict: de Marigny was not guilty. But while they didn't think de Marigny had killed Oakes, they did think he was not a model member of the community and ordered that he and a friend be deported from the country. The two were taken out of the Bahamas four days after the verdict was reached and sent to Cuba. Nancy went with him at first, and the two stayed with friend Ernest Hemingway. Inevitably, they separated in 1945 and divorced in 1949.

Nancy moved to Hollywood where she had an affair with actor Richard Greene, then married a German nobleman named Barron Ernst Lyssardt von Hoyingen-Huene, but they divorced in 1956. She died in 2005 and was survived by two children and two grandchildren. De Marigny remarried and died in 1998. Harold Christie was knighted in 1964 by Queen Elizabeth, niece to the Duke of Windsor. He died in 1973. The Duke himself was said to avoid all conversation about Oakes' death and became noticeably distraught whenever the subject came up. He died 1972.

Since de Marigny's acquittal, several conspiracy theories have emerged as to who might have killed Harry Oakes. While no one has ever again been charged with his murder, some of the conspiracy theories are more plausible than others. The most credible states that it was Harold Christie who killed Oakes. According to a timeline of events put together, Christie had been at a dinner party at the home the night before the night of the murder and had stayed overnight. He stayed the next day too, playing tennis and speaking with Oakes off and on. He testified the two went to bed at around 11:30, and he found Oakes' body the next morning. A couple of different reasons have been given to suspect him. Apparently, Christie had borrowed a large sum of money from Oakes, and Oakes was about to call the loan. Sometimes connected with this, and sometimes offered as a separate theory, was that Oakes was considering leaving the Bahamas for Mexico, and so Christie either killed him or did so with the help of his brother Frank.

Evidence has emerged in the years after the trial that seems to poke holes in Christie's testimony that he slept through the night and didn't leave the house. One Nassau police officer said that he spotted Christie driving a station wagon on the night of the murder. One book went so far as to offer the following information: at the time of Oakes' murder, only five station wagons were registered in New Providence. Of the five, one was owned by Christie, one by his brother Frank and one by Oakes' business manager Newell Kelly. There was evidence that Christie parked his car a considerable distance from Oakes' home. In addition, a night watchman claimed to have seen Christie and another man hanging around an unfamiliar boat at the Nassau harbour on the night of the murder. The night watchman was reported to have mysteriously drowned before the trial. Another theory purports that Christie killed Oakes with the help of de Marigny.

Several books have claimed that American gangsters killed Oakes over his opposition to bringing gambling to the islands. In some of the theories the head gangster is Meyer Lansky, an American gangster boss; in others it's the mafia, who used proxies to try to pressure Oakes into supporting casinos. In some scenarios Oakes initially agrees to take part but then withdraws his support, while in others he outright refuses to get involved. In some scenarios he is deliberately murdered to eliminate his opposition, while in others the death is accidental, the result of roughing him up but going too far. Some of these theories also feature Christie trying to get Oakes to support the idea of having casinos in the Bahamas. In the theory in which Oakes was accidentally killed by some gangsters trying to rough him up, it is Christie who helps return the body to Oakes' home to stage the scene of the murder. Some have said there were signs the crime scene may have been staged, such as blood flowing in directions it shouldn't be able to, but the evidence collected does not support this theory. These theories also usually report the complicity of the Duke of Windsor in covering up Oakes' death.

Others maintain it was still de Marigny and that only the skill of his defence attorney saved him from the gallows. One book claims that a Scotland Yard investigation four years after the trial concluded that de Marigny was in fact the murderer, but nothing has ever been made public. Some statements from the investigation seem to indicate that, when de Marigny was interviewed, he had singed hair on his forearm. While this may have been seen as evidence that he had burned himself when trying to light Oakes' bed and body on fire, he explained it away as either having occurred from smoking cigars or from cooking for his dinner guests.

Another theory has Oakes being killed after discovering corruption in the building of the Nassau International Airport. Oakes, this theory's proponents say, was scheduled to fly to Miami to make a statement, though why Oakes would fly to the U.S. to testify about construction corruption in the Bahamas is unknown.

More far-fetched theories claim that Oakes had somehow uncovered the secret Nazi roots of one of two possible individuals. The first was businessman Wenner-Gren, who lived on the island with his American wife and sold light bulbs and household electrical equipment. Apparently, Oakes may have discovered that he was a close friend of infamous Nazis such as Hermann Goering, and that Oakes was killed because he had unearthed information about the fact Wenner-Gren might have been a spy for the Germans.

The other person who is alleged to have had secret Nazi connections they were willing to kill to cover up is none other than the Duke of Windsor. This theory claims that the duke had previous dealings with the party and that Oakes had somehow uncovered evidence of these dealings.

One thing that was never established definitively was the weapon or tool that was used to kill Oakes. Again, various theories have been discussed, from a spiked club to a small-calibre gun to a boat's winch lever to a conch shell or just some other blunt object. Despite all the conjecture, one of the most important pieces of evidence—the murder weapon—was never uncovered by the authorities at the time or by anyone since.

While no solid evidence about who killed Harry Oakes has ever been revealed, there is no denying how rich he was at the time of his death. His estate, excluding the Lake Shore Gold Mine in Canada, was valued at $10.08 million. His income from the gold mine alone, between 1924 and 1943, after taxes, amounted to $34.7 million. When the mine was sold in February 1956, it had produced $250 million in gold and was estimated to have another 10 years worth of gold inside it.

Chapter 12

Lyle and Marie McCann

~

O f all the mysteries described in this book, this is the one with which I felt the greatest personal connection. In July 2010, I was an editor at the *St. Alberta Gazette* when Lyle and Marie McCann disappeared. The ensuing events have been equal portions mysterious, confusing and at times incomprehensible. A trial, if it actually gets to that stage, is still almost a year away. I cannot recall in all my years as a reporter, editor and author, a case in which, after so much time had passed since the person considered to be the main suspect was caught, that so little information has been shared with the public. The disappearance of this couple after they left their home in July 2010 definitely qualifies as one of the most compelling mysteries of modern times in Canada and in Alberta.

St. Albert, Alberta, is a bedroom community of Edmonton, the two cities essentially sharing a border. There are, at last count, about 65,000 people who call St. Albert home. Yet for a city of that size, violent crime is exceedingly rare. While

Edmonton typically counts a few dozen murders each year, St. Albert goes for years at a time without a murder reported. The only murder I covered as a reporter with the *Gazette* actually occurred outside the city, while the accused and convicted murderer was from St. Albert. Just to provide some context, here are the last few murders to have taken place:

- On Monday April 6, 2015, St. Albert RCMP found a 25-year-old man dead of gunshot wounds near an apartment complex in St. Albert. Police believe he had been shot in Edmonton then transported to St. Albert.

- On Saturday July 17, 2015, Shawn Maxwell Rehn shot RCMP officers Const. David Wynn and Aux. Const. Derek Bond at the casino. Const. Wynn died of his wounds after being taken off life support. Rehn's body was found later in the day. He is believed to have killed himself.

- Most notoriously, before the McCanns disappeared, St. Albert was mostly known as the city where Mark Twitchell, the Dexter killer, lived. In October 2008 he lured John Brian Altinger to a garage in Edmonton using a dating website, killed him then dismembered him. Twitchell was convicted of murder in 2011 and sentenced to life in prison.

- In February 2006, 63-year-old realtor William Maloney was stabbed to death by Lisa Ann McKay, a prostitute, in Maloney's St. Albert home. McKay pleaded guilty to manslaughter and served a six-year and five-month sentence.

So when information started coming in that an elderly couple from the city had disappeared, it was enough to get the entire community to stand up take notice. The events of July and August 2010 are entrenched in the memories of some residents of that city.

~

Lyle Thomas McCann was born August 24, 1931, near Red Deer, Alberta, one of six children. Marie Waltz was born October 14, 1932, in Torrington, Alberta. The two married in Torrington on July 30, 1952. They moved to St. Albert in 1964. Lyle worked as a long-haul truck driver, and they had three children. At the time they disappeared, Lyle was 78 years old and Marie was 77. Those that knew them described the pair as a loving couple.

"You would see them at night going for walks and holding hands and he used to call her darling," said long-time neighbour Norm Muffitt.

Here is what was supposed to happen. The McCanns were to leave St. Albert for Chilliwack, BC. They were scheduled to be in Abbotsford on July 10 to meet their daughter, who was flying into Abbotsford International Airport. The pair left St. Albert on July 3 in their 1999 Gulf Stream Voyager motor home pulling a light green Hyundai Tucson SUV. The last time they were seen alive was on July 3 at approximately 9:25 AM at the Superstore Gas Bar in St. Albert when they fuelled up their vehicle. They were scheduled to head west towards BC and were believed to be leaving the St. Albert and Edmonton area via the Yellowhead Highway.

No one ever saw or heard from them again.

On July 5, the RCMP in Edson, a town at the base of the Rocky Mountains, on the Yellowhead Highway, were called to the scene of a vehicle fire at the Minnow Lake campground nearby. When the vehicle was extinguished, they found it was a motor home. Further investigation revealed that the motor home belonged to a Lyle and Marie McCann, who at that time were not considered missing. The green Hyundai Tucson was not at the campground. The RCMP tried to call the phone number found for the McCanns but got no answer. They contacted the St. Albert RCMP detachment and asked them to try and contact the couple at their home. The RCMP went to the McCann home in St. Albert, but no one answered the door. It's not clear what, if anything, the RCMP did afterwards to try and contact the McCanns.

July 10 came, and Lyle and Marie McCann did not arrive in Abbotsford as scheduled. Their daughter, Trudy Holder, notified the RCMP that the couple was missing, and a missing persons notification was issued for them. When the RCMP started their investigation, they quickly learned about the discovery of the couple's burning motor home at the Minnow Lake campground. On July 12, the RCMP disclosed to the public what had happened with the discovery of the motor home and were met with instant criticism that they had not done more at the time the burning motor home had been found.

"It is a crime, but it was not that serious a crime because it was a property crime, not a person crime," RCMP Sergeant Patrick Webb was quoted as saying about why the police didn't do more when the motor home was found. "In a perfect world those steps would have been taken right away, but we just can't do that with every burned vehicle. I myself have probably done a dozen of those over my career."

The police announced they had launched aerial and ground searches of the area around Edson and that they were checking the McCann's bank records and cell phone records to see if there had been any recent activity. The family offered that they thought the couple was planning to spend the first night of their trip in Blue River, BC.

"Our family is just devastated, from my father and mother's siblings to my brother and sister and our children. It is just devastating us all. I am hoping that they maybe got waylaid, maybe the Hyundai got stuck somewhere. I am hoping they're out there somewhere in the bush," their son, Bret McCann, was quoted as saying in the press.

Very soon after the announcement of the discovery of the burned motor home, the RCMP announced that they were conducting a review into exactly what had happened when the force discovered who owned the burned motor home.

"When the motor home was burnt initially we were slow getting going as information wasn't passed on and a couple of things weren't followed up on," Assistant Commissioner Peter Hourihan said, conceding that the RCMP made some mistakes.

"The whole thing is under review. We are talking to [them], saying what did you do, when did you do it and if any of that leads into St. Albert then we are going there and looking into that as well," Webb said.

The RCMP were also still looking for the green Hyundai Tucson, hoping that tracking down the SUV might lead them if not to the McCanns, then to information about what had happened to them. But even this line of inquiry ran into problems. The RCMP received a tip that the SUV had been seen in Prince George, but the employee that took the call didn't write down the contact information for the tipster. The RCMP was forced to issue a plea through the media for that person to return to the police station, which they did two days later.

But the SUV wasn't found in Prince George. It was later reported that the SUV was found Friday, July 16 near Edson, the town near the site of the burned-out motor home. At first the RCMP wouldn't say publicly where they found the SUV, maintaining the SUV and the area around it were a crime scene. At the same time, they also announced that they had identified a person of interest. That person was identified as a 38-year-old male named Travis Edward Vader.

A quick look at Vader's criminal history had a lot of people wondering why the RCMP were only referring to him as a person of interest, but the police refused to call him a suspect.

"Vader has multiple outstanding warrants on matters unrelated to this, and he is known to be in possession of firearms. He has a history of drug abuse," Hourihan said.

Hourihan was blunt about what the RMCP believed had happened to the McCanns.

"We suspect foul play. Everyone can draw their own conclusions. This is completely out of character for them not to have contacted anyone or arrived to pick up their daughter. We assume the worst and hope for the best," Hourihan said, adding the RCMP were still looking for anyone who might have seen the SUV or motor home between July 3 and July 5 to come forward.

On July 19, the RCMP arrested Vader in dramatic fashion. Members of the RCMP Emergency Response Team (ERT) descended on a house near MacKay, Alberta, northwest of Edson, and stormed it in the early morning hours. Inside they found Vader and one other man, who was also taken into custody. The other man was later released without charge.

Vader made a court appearance on July 27 that was covered by much of the media from the Edmonton area. The full litany of criminal charges Vader was facing at that time was laid bare. He was wanted for offences in Barrhead, Mayerthorpe, Edson, Edmonton, Evansburg and St. Albert. Those charges included weapons and drug offences, possession of stolen property, mischief and arson. Specifically in St. Albert he had been charged with driving while unauthorized and driving without a licence. He had skipped out on a June 25 court date on those charges, and a warrant had been issued for his arrest.

A website and Facebook page were set up for the couple. On July 24, the family hosted a candlelight vigil for the two. Some 250 people were estimated to attend.

Yet next to no information was forthcoming as to how the RCMP had come to determine Vader was a person of interest, nor what they thought had actually happened to Lyle and Marie. They continued their searches in the area, first checking a campground near Nojack, which was close to MacKay, where Vader had been found. The tips were rolling in, too. By late July the RCMP had received 470 tips from the public, but that volume slowed to a trickle as time passed. In early August, the family and supporters started putting up posters in northwest Edmonton, hoping that doing so might pry loose an important piece of information.

"Someone, somewhere has some information and can help the police find my parents and bring them home safe," Bret McCann told the media. The family even set up a trust fun for the couple, hoping they might be able to use the funds to somehow find their parents.

"We have ideas, but whatever we do we want to do something that is complementary to what the police are doing," Bret said.

The family continued their search for information about their parents. They attended a court hearing for Vader in Edmonton to try and get a look at him, but Vader's lawyer appeared for him. They sent posters to the Edson area, asking people living in the area to check their properties for any signs of the couple. In mid-August, the family announced it was offering a reward for anyone with information that might help bring the family home. They had already received a $10,000 anonymous donation to go with the $1000 accumulated in the trust fund. They partnered with the City of St. Albert to set up the reward. Within three days, the value of the reward had grown to $30,000 as more and more donations came in, including two valued at $10,000.

"We have always known that there is a huge amount of support out there in our parents and in their plight, so it is very gratifying," said Bret.

On September 1, the RCMP confirmed what many had already come to believe. Vader was now considered a suspect instead of just a person of interest. The distinction is quite important. A person of interest is someone who is believed to know something or have been a witness to a crime. A suspect is believed to have committed the crime. The news offered little comfort to the family.

"I am infuriated, basically knowing that Travis Vader could have known where my parents are and hasn't said anything all summer," Bret McCann said. "How could someone know something about a pair of elderly people in the woods and keep that information to themselves?"

The reward pot continued to grow, reaching $50,000 and then being capped at $60,000. The family announced that the total of the reward would grow no higher.

The RCMP still searched for the McCanns, but they said even less about the case than earlier. They searched a rural property near Nojack, even calling in a dive team to search a small pond on the property. By September 15, the RCMP wrapped up their search. Little information was released about what exactly the RCMP were looking for on the property.

The McCann family then took some of the investigation into their own hands, starting their own search of Crown lands in the area where both vehicles were found.

"The police can't be everywhere, and we are trying to help them by doing our own search," said Bret McCann. " We are trying to carefully go down every road and every place we think a vehicle might have gone through."

Every weekend, members of the family headed out to the area in their vehicles, searching every bridge, creek and culvert.

"We have wanted to come forever, but originally the RCMP didn't want anyone out here, and I understand that. They didn't want anyone trampling over something that could be something, but two-and-a half months later, a cigarette butt isn't going to be affected by us," said nephew Murray McCann.

They mounted platforms on their vehicles so they could see a little farther into the bush. They were forced to limit their search to areas they felt their vehicles could reach, but they tried to talk with as many people as they could in an effort to jog their memories. They took posters with them and fastened them to fences in the hopes of stirring fresh memories. In late October, the family purchased space on a roadside billboard along the Yellowhead Highway.

"We wanted to reinforce it in the public mind, especially those people who live in that area and frequently travel along Highway 16," said Bret McCann. The family even paired with local sporting good stores to provide information to hunters in the area who were purchasing their licences.

By Christmas, there was little news to report. The RCMP had interviewed more than 200 people, searched 30 properties, collected 1400 documents and still had 20 investigators working full time on the case.

Vader was still in custody, even though he hadn't yet been charged with anything related to the McCanns' disappearance. In March 2011, Vader applied for bail but was denied. The reasons were kept private under a publication ban granted by the judge. This particular hearing marked the third time Vader tried to get out on bail and was refused.

At that point, the family was just looking for closure.

"We have come to accept that something awful happened to my parents," Bret said. "We just need to know what happened to my parents."

A brief flurry of activity occurred in June 2011 when the RCMP launched a search of a rural property near Lodgepole, located 180 kilometres southwest of Edmonton and well away from the area where all previous searches had taken place. They even went so far as to solicit help from the Brazeau Regional Search and Rescue Society, but the search wrapped up with no new information being made public.

By late July 2011, more than year after their parents had first disappeared, the McCanns placed an obituary in local papers for their parents and planned a memorial service for them at St. Albert Catholic Parish. Before the service took place, a judge took the step of declaring the McCanns legally dead.

"It's been over a year now, and we realize our parents must be gone. So this is what we're trying to do, to move towards closure now," Bret said.

But although they accepted their parents were dead, the family was still determined to find out what happened to them, and in October 2011 renewed their efforts, passing out flyers to Edson-area hunting stores that could in turn be handed out to hunters coming in for their licenses.

"Hunting season is opening again, and my parents have still not been found, so we are going to make a plea to hunters to keep an eye out for anything unusual," Bret McCann said, adding the police thought that hunters might notice something, like land that had been disturbed.

Vader was still in jail and still in the news. His lawyer had been preparing to challenge Vader's continued incarceration on constitutional grounds, but then announced he would be abandoning that strategy. Vader asserted that he was having a rough time in custody, accusing guards at the Edmonton Remand Centre of beating him and saying he was being treated poorly because of his notoriety as a result of the McCann case. He and his lawyer claimed video evidence of the guards assaulting him, but when the footage was reviewed in court, all that was visible was the guards escorting Vader out of the camera frame. He claimed the assault took place shortly after he walked out of the frame.

On April 2, 2012, after more than a year and a half of investigating, Vader, now 40, was officially charged with two counts of first-degree murder in the deaths of Lyle and Marie McCann. He was arrested at the Edmonton Remand Centre and charged.

"We are very optimistic that this will bring us one step closer to finding out what happened to our parents," said Bret after the news was announced.

On October 20, 2012, Vader caught a bit of a break when the eight drug and firearms charges he was facing were thrown out because of a mistrial. The judge believed a mistrial was required when it came to light that the Crown was in possession of some evidence that it had not shared with the defence. By January 2013, Vader was recommitted to trial on the same charges.

On July 13, 2013, the Crown announced it was cancelling the preliminary inquiry and was filing a direct indictment against Vader, which would send the case immediately to trial. The accused is usually given the option of first having a preliminary inquiry, where a judge hears the Crown's evidence and decides whether or not there is enough evidence to warrant a trial.

In February 2014, Vader announced he was suing the RCMP for $150,000. The exact reason was difficult to discern, but according to the statement of claim, a man named Thomas Berube had provided Vader a letter of employment. Berube was accused of being an agent of the RCMP and the letter fraudulent. This was done so that the RCMP could use the charges against him as a delaying tactic and they would not have to release him from custody. Vader claimed that he didn't know the letter was a fake, and he was, as a result of the letter, charged with obstruction of justice and uttering forged documents. The charges were dropped, before he was scheduled to stand trial.

But the biggest shock came the following month. On March 22, 2014, the Crown announced that it would stay the first-degree murder charges against Vader. A stay is not the same as withdrawing charges against someone. A stay simply puts charges on hold, and the Crown can bring those charges back against the accused within a year of the stay being entered. But a stay is often a precursor to charges being withdrawn, so the announcement had the effect of a bombshell being dropped on Edmonton and St. Albert. Vader's lawyer, Brian Beresh, was heavily critical of the Crown and RCMP.

"They named him as a suspect, which we say was not based on any reliable evidence. Then when it came time for trial, there was no reliable evidence, and this was an easy way out for them," Beresh said.

The McCann family released a statement saying they didn't think the case was necessarily finished.

"Though we see this as a delay in our search for justice, our family remains confident that the ongoing investigation will lead to the conclusion in this matter."

Vader wasted no time filing a lawsuit on April 26, 2014, against 60 different people including Crown prosecutors, the RCMP and the attorney general of Canada. He alleged abuse of authority, malicious prosecution and mistreatment by correctional officers, sheriffs and police informants. He claimed that the RCMP and the Crown had deliberately prolonged his prosecution on the first-degree murder charges despite having no reasonable likelihood of conviction. The total value of the lawsuit was $1 million. But Vader still wasn't free. He was again denied bail, this time on charges of theft, drug trafficking, careless storage of a firearm and a breach of a recognizance.

On October 8, 2014, Vader was actually acquitted of nine separate charges that he was facing.

But any celebration over his acquittal was short-lived. On December 19, 2014, Vader was re-arrested and charged with the first-degree murders of Lyle and Marie McCann. Yet despite the unexpected development, neither the Crown nor the RCMP divulged anything publicly that justified bringing back the charges that had been stayed. Only one comment from the Crown offered any insight into what had happened. Apparently there had been an issue with disclosure of evidence that led to the stay of charges in March. Since that time, the Crown said, additional information had come to light that justified bringing back the charges.

"We will now have the opportunity to learn more about the investigation into our parents' death when this case comes to trial. Our goal now is to ensure the accused receives a fair trial," said the McCanns in a statement issued to the media.

Even with the charges against him, Vader was actually released on $25,000 bail and ordered confined to his home. In late January, a date for trial was finally set. Travis Vader will stand trial in the murders of Lyle and Marie McCann on March 3, 2016. The trial is expected to last a month or more. When asked, Vader elected to have his trial heard by both a judge and a jury instead of only a judge.

"We are relieved that this is finally going ahead and 2016 seems a long way away, but it will come, " the McCann family said.

But Vader continued to make headlines. On February 12, 2015, Vader was arrested by the RCMP in St. Albert and taken into custody after the police were called to the home where he was serving his house arrest. He was subsequently charged with assault and failing to comply with a condition of his release to keep the peace and be of good behaviour. The assault apparently involved an altercation with his mother's boyfriend.

He was released again on bail and managed to stay out the news for a few weeks when he was arrested yet again. This time, the police were called to a residence near Carrot Creek, about 35 minutes east of Edson, at 10:30 PM on Saturday, February 28. The owner of the residence noticed a strange vehicle in the driveway but didn't recognize the truck and couldn't identify the driver. The property owner called the police when the truck hadn't moved for some time. The police arrived and found Vader inside the truck. He was charged with dangerous operation of a motor vehicle and six counts of failing to comply with the conditions of his bail, specifically the conditions not to possess any firearms, ammunition, explosives or weapons; not to have contact with a specific individual and not to be in possession of non-prescription drugs. He was again granted bail on April 11, 2015, and released but this time under heavier conditions. He was to wear an electronic monitoring bracelet, abide by a curfew of between 10:00 PM to 6:00 AM and he was not to possess firearms, ammunition or explosives and not to have contact with several specific people.

In an interview with the *Edmonton Journal* after his arrest in Carrot Creek but before he was released from custody, Vader and his fiancée Sheila Gangl said the RCMP were harassing Vader and were looking for any reason to make him look bad. Vader asserted that no assault took place in the February 12 incident that involved his mother's boyfriend. In the Carrot Creek incident, Vader and Gangl said they were driving in the area when they pulled over to watch the northern lights. The RCMP promptly showed up and arrested them at gunpoint.

"Even before these charges, they were harassing him," said Gangl.

The weapon discovered in their possession was, said the pair, Gangl's fishing knife, and the drug allegation had to do with a package of plastic windshield wiper tubing the police thought was used to consume methamphetamine.

"They're trying to charge him with anything, obviously. I was there, and I know for a fact what happened," Gangl said.

Vader went so far as to state he felt the RCMP were looking for an opportunity to kill him.

"I honestly think they are looking for a chance to shoot me," he said. "If we would have made one wrong move that night, we both would've been shot."

On April 18, one week after his release on the Carrot Creek charges, Vader was arrested in Camrose at St. Mary's Hospital and charged with failing to comply with the conditions of his release. Information from his electronic monitoring bracelet showed that he was driving on Highway 21 north of Camrose when he was supposed to be observing his curfew. It was noted that he had been in the Wabamun area (west of Edmonton) just before his curfew. The police tried talking to Vader through his bracelet, but Vader didn't respond. While his bail conditions allowed him to break curfew in the event of a medical emergency, the police revealed that his trip to St. Mary's Hospital didn't qualify as a medical emergency, even though he apparently was there to seek medical treatment. He was released from custody the following day, and two weeks later the Crown dropped the charges stemming from this particular incident, stating it was not in the public's interest to proceed.

On June 13, 2015, Vader was arrested in Barrhead, Alberta. He was reported at the time to be facing "multiple charges for two alleged assaults." The police later said he was charged as a result of a "spousal assault allegation." In total, Vader was charged with two counts of assault and six counts of failing to comply with his bail conditions. One assault was alleged to have taken place in April, while the other took place in June. The victim in both assaults was the same person.

Barring any future developments, Travis Vader will stand trial for the murders of Lyle and Marie McCann in March 2016, almost six years after they disappeared. Vader is presumed innocent until proven guilty, and the bodies of Lyle and Marie McCann, presuming they are deceased, have not been found at the time of this writing.

Saskatchewan Petroglyphs

~

The province of Saskatchewan in and of itself might not strike most people as mysterious. But there are a series of markings on stones throughout the province for which little explanation has been provided.

Petroglyphs are images that have been carved into rock. They typically date back anywhere from hundreds to thousands of years ago. Saskatchewan actually has several sites featuring petroglyphs from Canada's past.

Most notable are the petroglyphs at St. Victor, a small town just east of Assiniboia. In fact, more than 300 images have been carved onto a sandstone outcropping known as Ravenscrag. The images are of unknown origin but feature changes in style that indicate the carvings might stretch over a long period of time. The carvings, which have been dated at anywhere from 300 to 1000 years old, feature figures of bison, turtles, human heads, footprints and handprints, as well as water creatures and stars, among others. Popular thinking is that the images may have been a way of bringing about a certain kind of magic, or that they may be the record of a dream or vision quest.

The Herschel petroglyphs are also well known. These are a series of dots, circles and lines that have been carved into a limestone boulder for what are believed to be ceremonial purposes dating back as far as 1000 years ago. It has been suggested that the markings represent the hoof prints of buffalo. The First Nations consider the site to be sacred.

Once located in Riverhurst but now preserved in the Moose Jaw Museum, there is also a stone that features the image of a human face. One mark across the forehead of the face seems to indicate the person in the image is wearing a hood.

The Royal Saskatchewan Museum in Regina also features a petroglyph of a human face. It was originally discovered in 1912 in the hills northeast of Fort Qu'Apelle.

Truax is also home to a petroglyph of a face, but this stone features a face on both the front of the stone and the back.

The mystery of who carved these images and when may never be solved, but the their presence is an eerie glance into our country's distant past.

Notes on Sources

~

The Franklin Expedition

Atwood, Margaret. "Haunted By a Face." *National Post*. October 2, 2004. B1.

Simpson, John Worsley. "Behind Ever Great Man is a Great Woman: History." *National Post*. December 17, 2005. WP17.

Boswell, Randy. "Inuit oral history alters lore of Franklin; 1850 Arctic Tragedy." *National Post*. June 26, 2008. A2.

"Canada to embark on its biggest search for fabled British shipwrecks." *National Post*. August 5, 2008. A7.

Boswell, Randy. "Search for Franklin shipwrecks to proceed." *National Post*. August 16, 2008. A8.

"Archaeologists pick up clues off Arctic coast in search for British shipwrecks." *National Post*. August 27, 2008. A5.

Boswell, Randy. "Expert hopes to cap legacy." *National Post*. September 4, 2008. A9.

"Ships clock supposedly lost in failed 19th-century Arctic expedition resurfaces." *National Post*. May 21, 2009. A8.

"'Off the scale' lead levels found in 160-year-old Arctic soup can." *National Post*. December 16, 2009. A9.

Martin, Don. "Ship intact, upright in isolated bay." *National Post*. July 28, 2010. A1.

Martin, Don. "Investigating shipwreck was worth the cost." *National Post*. August 3, 2010. A6.

Prentice, Jim. "Reclaiming a piece of our history." *National Post*. August 10, 2010. A15.

Boswell, Randy. "Science thaws cold case." *National Post*. March 22, 2011. A3.

Hopper, Tristan. "Ice, terror & darkness." *National Post*. July 5, 2011. A4.

Boswell, Randy. "Arctic hunt for sunken ships to continue." *National Post*. September 2, 2011. A8.

"Long lost ships: What the #!%*?." *National Post*. August 24, 2012. A4.

Moore, Dene. "Search for Franklin Expedition yields remains." *National Post*. September 10, 2012. A1.

Brewster, Murray. "Harper visits Franklin expedition searchers." *National Post*. August 23, 2013. A4.

Long, Kat. "Franklin Fever." *National Post*. May 22, 2014. A13.

Den Tandt. Michael. "Mining the depths of Franklin mystery." *National Post*. August 26, 2014. A3.

Blanchfield, Mike and Rennie, Steve. "How the missing ship was found." *National Post*. September 10, 2014. A6.

Humphreys, Adrian. "With Franklin find, PM's Arctic Ship comes in." *National Post*. September 10, 2014. A1.

Spears, Tom. "Team set to dive on Franklin site." *National Post*. September 11, 2014. A6.

Rennie, Steve. "Franklin ship found in Arctic is HMS Erebus." *National Post*. October 2, 2014. A7.

Winter, Kathleen. "Finder of the Arctic's secrets." *National Post*. October 9, 2014. A16.

"Bell salvaged from Franklin wreck unveiled." *National Post*. November 7, 2014. A6.

Tom Thomson

Welcome. (n.d.). Retrieved February 13, 2015, from http://www.canadianmysteries.ca/sites/thomson/home/indexen.html

Tom Thomson. (n.d.). Retrieved February 13, 2014, from http://en.wikipedia.org/wiki/Tom_Thomson

The Black Donnellys

The Official Donnelly Home Page. (n.d.). Retrieved February 17, 2014, from http://www.donnellys.com

Black Donnellys. (n.d.). Retrieved February 17, 2014, from http://en.wikipedia.org/wiki/Black_Donnellys

Welcome. (n.d.). Retrieved March 2, 2014, from http://www.canadianmysteries.ca/sites/norman/home/indexen.html

Oak Island

Oak Island. (n.d.). Retrieved February 4, 2014. fromhttp://en.wikipedia.org/wiki/Oak_Island

Treasure: Oak Island: The Story of Oak Island. (n.d.). Retrieved February 4, 2014, from http://www.activemind.com/Mysterious/topics/oakisland/story.html

OAK ISLAND Treasure Pit / Money Pit. (2014, October 30). from http://www.mysteriesofcanada.com/nova-scotia/oak-island-treasure-pit/

E. Herbert Norman

Kramer, John (1998). *The Man Who Might Have Been: An Inquiry into the Life and Death of Herbert Norman.* National Film Board.

Jerome

Jerome. (n.d.). Retrieved April 3, 2014, from http://www.canadianmysteries.ca/sites/jerome/suites/souvenir/3614en.html

Gerald Bull

(1991) *The Man Who Made the Supergun.* Public Broadcasting Service.

Gerald Bull. (n.d.). Retrieved May 9, 2014, from http://en.wikipedia.org/wiki/Gerald_Bull

The Granger Affair

The Strange Disappearance of Granger Taylor | Mysterious Universe. (n.d.). Retrieved May 13, 2014, from http://mysteriousuniverse.org/2012/10/the-strange-disappearance-of-granger-taylor/

Is Vanished Son Adrift In Space? (n.d.). Retrieved May 14, 2014, from http://www.ufobc.ca/Reports/Collection/collection18mar85.htm

"Bones may be those UFO fan who 'blasted off.'" *Montreal Gazette.* March 31, 1986.

William Robinson

Welcome. (n.d.). Retrieved May 9, 2014, from http://www.canadianmysteries.ca/sites/robinson/home/indexen.html

Peter Verigin

Peter Verigin history. (n.d.). Retrieved May 12, 2014, from http://www.canadian-mysteries.ca/sites/verigin/context/peterverigin/indexen.html

Peter Verigin. (n.d.). Retrieved May 14, 2014, from http://en.wikipedia.org/wiki/Peter_Verigin

Harry Oakes

Harry Oakes. (n.d.). Retrieved May 1, 2014, from http://en.wikipedia.org/wiki/Harry_Oakes

Boyd, William. "The real-life murder behind Any Human Heart." (November 13, 2010). Retrieved May 1, 2014, from http://www.theguardian.com/culture/2010/nov/13/william-boyd-any-human-heart-murder

Niagara Falls - Sir Harry Oakes: A History. (n.d.). Retrieved May 1, 2015, from http://www.niagarafrontier.com/oakes.html

Lyle and Marie McCann

Tumilty, Ryan. "Missing couple's motor home destroyed by fire." *St. Albert Gazette*. July 14, 2010. 1.

Tumilty, Ryan. "RCMP under scrutiny." *St. Albert Gazette*. July 17, 2010. 4.

Tumilty, Ryan. "Missing couple's SUV found." *St. Albert Gazette*. July 17, 2010. 1.

Tumilty, Ryan. "Vader caught." *St. Albert Gazette*. July 21, 2010. 1.

Tumilty, Ryan. "Candlelight vigil planned for missing couple." *St. Albert Gazette*. July 24, 2010. 1.

Tumilty, Ryan. "Community rallies behind McCann family at vigil." *St. Albert Gazette*. July 28, 2010. 1.

Tumilty, Ryan. "McCann family plasters Edmonton in posters." *St. Albert Gazette*. August 4, 2010. 1.

Tumilty, Ryan. "Reward offered for couple's return." *St. Albert Gazette*. August 18, 2010. 1.

Tumilty, Ryan. "Reward fund swells in first few days." *St. Albert Gazette*. August 21, 2010. 1.

Tumilty, Ryan. "Search ends on rural property in McCann investigation." *St. Albert Gazette*. September 15, 2010. 1.

Tumilty, Ryan. "McCann family refuses to rest." *St. Albert Gazette*. October 6, 2010. 3.

Tumilty, Ryan. "RCMP conduct search in McCann case." *St. Albert Gazette*. June 29, 2011. 1.

Tumilty, Ryan. "McCanns hope obit, service bring closure." *St. Albert Gazette.* July 23, 2011. 1.

Tumilty, Ryan. "Judge declares McCanns legally dead." *St. Albert Gazette.* July 27, 2011. 1.

Tumilty, Ryan and Sarrazin, Megan. "Travis Vader charged in McCann deaths." *St. Albert Gazette.* April 25, 2012. 1.

Crofts, Amy. "Double murder goes straight to trial." *St. Albert Gazette.* July 13, 2013. 3.

Crofts, Amy. "Accused killer sues RCMP." *St. Albert Gazette.* February 15, 2014. 10.

Crofts, Amy. "Charges stayed in McCann murder case." *St. Albert Gazette.* March 22, 2014. 1.

Crofts, Amy. "Vader files suit for $1 million." *St. Albert Gazette.* April 26, 2014. 3.

Crofts, Amy. "Travis Vader recharged with McCann murder." *St. Albert Gazette.* December 24, 2014. 5.

Crofts, Amy. "Vader to be released on house arrest." *St. Albert Gazette.* December 27, 2014. 7.

Pruss, Viola. "Vader trial set." *St. Albert Gazette.* January 24, 2015. 5.

Pruss, Viola. "Vader back in custody." *St. Albert Gazette.* February 18, 2015. 1.

Pruss, Viola. "Vader arrested near Carrot Creek." *St. Albert Gazette.* March 4, 2015. 5.

Pruden, Jana. "Vader, fiancée, allege RCMP harassment in latest charges." *Edmonton Journal.* March 10, 2015.

Pruss, Viola. "Vader granted bail, again." *St. Albert Gazette.* April 11, 2015. 6.

Pruss, Viola. "Vader arrested for third time this year." *St. Albert Gazette.* April 18, 2015. 14.

"Vader charge dropped." *St. Albert Gazette.* May 2, 2015. 22.

About the Author

~

Bestselling author and award-winning journalist Peter Boer has served as reporter and co-editor for the *St. Albert Gazette*. He has a degree in psychology from the University of Alberta in Edmonton and a graduate diploma in journalism from Concordia University in Montréal. In his commitment to lifelong learning, he has taken another leap in his career, having graduated with a Bachelor of Education. He will now be teaching the finer points of writing to his students. He has a dozen other books to his credit including *Canadian Crime Investigations: Hunting Down Serial Killers, Fallen Officers: Canadian Police in the Line of Fire* and *Wrongfully Convicted: The Innocent in Canada for Quagmire Press.*

Check out more Mysteries from

QUAGMIRE PRESS

MYSTERIOUS ALBERTA
Myths, Murders, Mysteries and Legends

by Lisa Wojna

Alberta has a dark underbelly that is rife with legends, hauntings, unsolved crimes and unexplained events:

• Somewhere in southwestern Alberta is a pot of gold known as the Lost Lemon Mine, if you can get past the curse; no one has ever been able to find the location

• The Atlas Coal Mine near Drumheller has its fair share of strange mysteries—why did a mine manager make sure no one else could access the contents of the office safe, which remains locked to this day?

Read about these and other unexplained events in *Mysterious Alberta*.

$18.95 • 978-1-926695-21-1 • 5.25" x 8.25" • 256 pages

MYSTERIOUS BRITISH COLUMBIA
Myths, Murders, Mysteries and Legends

by Valerie Green

Crimes never solved, eerie sightings never explained, and paranormal events to stretch the limits of the mind—read about the mysteries that continue to baffle British Columbians to this day.

$18.95 • 978-1-926695-18-1 • 5.25" x 8.25" • 256 pages

MYSTERIOUS ONTARIO
Myths, Murders, Mysteries and Legends

by Geordie Telfer

Ontario's history is brimming with mysteries. From the dawn of pre-history to the present, unexplained events have confounded everyone from First Nations founders to present-day 24-hour news junkies. Unlock the past as you discover Ontario's secret history of unsolved disappearances, ghostly encounters, UFO abductions and more.

$18.95 • ISBN 978-1-926695-17-4 • 5.25" x 8.25" • 256 pages

Available from your local bookseller or by contacting the distributor, Lone Pine Publishing
1-800-661-9017
www.lonepinepublishing.com